NO ONE CAN STOP ME

But Me

A Journey from Childhood Trauma to a Life of Abundance

JENNIFER HERNANDEZ

with Glenn Plaskin

Forefront
BOOKS

NO ONE CAN STOP ME BUT ME:
A Journey from Childhood Trauma to a Life of Abundance

Published by Forefront Books.
Distributed by Simon & Schuster.

Library of Congress Control Number: 2023916824

Print ISBN: 978-1- 63763-205-5
E-book ISBN: 978-1-63763-206-2

Cover Design by Bruce Gore, Gore Studio, Inc.
Interior Design by Mary Susan Oleson, BLU Design Concepts

TO MY MOTHER AND MY FATHER, who coped so valiantly with a child as rebellious as me! But there are no regrets. If anything had happened differently, I would not be who I am today, able to impact others and set an example for what is possible when we choose to believe in ourselves.

I also dedicate this book to my four children, Mikey, Destiny, Damien, and Angelina. None of what I accomplished would have been possible without each of you. You are my strength and inspiration for it all . . . love you.

CONTENTS

FOREWORD BY RYAN BLAIR

WHEN I FIRST MET Jennifer Hernandez, I saw in her eyes the same fire that once consumed me—a relentless desire to rise above circumstances, to shatter the glass ceilings imposed by society, and most importantly, to make the world a better place. Over the years as her mentor in both business and life, I've had the privilege of witnessing her grow from a woman burdened by her past to an unstoppable force of nature.

Jennifer is not just another entrepreneur; she's a visionary. Her journey, as you will read in the pages that follow, is nothing short of miraculous. It's a testament to the indomitable human spirit, the power of resilience, and the transformative magic of relentless self-belief. I've mentored many people in my life, but few have taken the teachings to heart the way Jennifer has. She doesn't just listen; she applies, she evolves, and she conquers.

In the business world, Jennifer has shown an uncanny ability to adapt and thrive. Whether it was navigating the treacherous waters of the mortgage industry or building a team that reflects her own drive and commitment, she has proven time and again that she is a leader in every sense of the word. Her achievements in business are not just about financial gains;

they are about ethical victories and proving that success can be achieved without compromising on one's values.

What truly sets Jennifer apart is her spiritual journey—her quest to find a higher purpose in life. As her spiritual mentor, I've seen her grapple with the existential questions that plague us all: Why am I here? What is my purpose? How can I serve? And I've seen her find her answers, not in the material world, but in the realm of the spirit. Her deep-rooted desire to make a positive impact, to leave the world better than she found it, is what makes her story so compelling and inspiring.

Jennifer's life is a masterclass in transformation. It's a story that proves that no matter where you come from, no matter what obstacles you face, you have the power to dictate your own destiny. As you delve into her narrative, I hope you find not just inspiration but also the courage to take control of your own life, to break free from your limitations, and to strive for a world that reflects the beauty of your dreams

In the end, Jennifer's story is not just her own. It's a story that belongs to all of us, a mirror that reflects our collective potential to transform, to love, and to heal. And for that, I am incredibly proud to have been a part of her journey and to introduce you to the extraordinary life of Jennifer Hernandez.

Here's to the unstoppable spirit in all of us.

Ryan Blair, CEO, AlterCall
#1 *NEW YORK TIMES* BESTSELLING AUTHOR

Family Split Apart

IN A WORLD FULL of battles, the biggest one you'll ever face is the one *within* you.

My life is a testimony to the fact that you can survive and even thrive as you recover from setbacks that seemed impossible to overcome.

My early childhood story was one of suffering, sacrifice, and family trauma. Yet with perseverance and resilience, I ultimately found a path toward prosperity and a happy family life. I consider this turnaround the ultimate triumph. But it wasn't easy getting there.

As you'll read, my life was plagued by sexual promis- cuity, drugs, guns, alcohol, and gang violence. It was a dark existence of self-sabotage and self-degradation. I could easily have ended up with my name in an obituary.

The odds were certainly stacked against me.

It was only when I got pregnant at nineteen that I finally knew I had to make a real change to protect the life of my soon-to-be-born baby. Yet even *then*, because of the choices I had made up to that point, I found it incredibly difficult to change my habits and get away from a self-destructive way of life.

What happens when you are all alone with no one to turn to? Do you crumble and fall? Or do you stand up and fight? For me, the only way I could possibly survive was to fight *back*. So instead of giving in to defeat, I fought for my baby's life—and for my own. Fighting for yourself—and not giving up—is the hardest battle ever.

But because of my baby, I instinctively knew I had to pull myself together; I soon realized that if I was still *living*, I must have a *purpose*.

It was in that moment of realization that I began to change my ways.

Thankfully, I found a power within me that kept me strong enough to keep on fighting. With nobody to turn to, I turned *within*, but that was a lonely path. I eventually began reaching out to others, and once I did, my life began to transform.

This is a preview of what is to come—a story of strength and determination, a testament to hope, even when there was nothing left to hope for, even when I gave everything and still had nothing.

For those reading this today who may feel overwhelmed, or unworthy, or too weak to overcome life's challenges, I hope this book will give you enough strength to stay strong and keep trying.

As I've learned, perseverance trumps every obstacle. Where there is faith, there is hope. Where there is darkness, there is a possibility of light.

Can you do it?

I am here to tell you that you can. If I can make it through with the odds stacked against me, then you can do it too.

Here is my story.

Part One

CHAPTER ONE

Helium Wonders

October 20, 2010
New Lenox, Illinois

I JUST CAN'T . . . I cannot do this anymore, I thought as I began to cry.

At age thirty-two, my fears had overwhelmed me. And the only thought that came to my mind was that there must be more to life than this—more than such a profound sense of sadness and defeat, feeling so lost and alone. How could this be?

After all, there I was, sitting in a half-million-dollar house in suburban New Lenox, a beautiful home my husband and I had built five years earlier. In the background, I could hear the laughing voices of my four-year-old twins playing in the other room; meanwhile, my husband was outside with the neighbors, having drinks and playing bean bags as if everything was okay.

But it was not okay at all. Everything felt wrong. The

conflicts and dilemmas within were tearing me apart. And it seemed as if nothing was ever going to change. My life was at a standstill.

It felt as if a storm had been brewing inside me for months. And on this day, that storm erupted, with tears pouring from my eyes. I couldn't see straight, and my head was pounding. My sobs were so wrenching that I couldn't catch my breath. I thought, *Is this really how my life is supposed to be? After everything I have overcome, is this the result? Is this really it?*

I hung my head in shame for even entertaining the extremely ungrateful thoughts that were consuming me. I felt lost and alone, overwhelmingly sad and defeated. In fact, at this point in my existence, I was so consistently depressed that I would often sit on the floor and just cry. I was so dysfunctional that our house was chronically dirty. In my state of mind, I just couldn't keep up with it.

And that's when I saw a yellow spiral notebook, casually left on the kitchen counter by one of my children. It looked as lonely and abandoned as I felt.

I reached for that book, intending to write a letter to my kids about what I had been through and how much I had overcome. I wanted to explain to them *why* I was having such a difficult time handling my day-to-day emotions. Though the material circumstances of my life were now so abundant, I couldn't shake off the ripple effects of my past, which is why I wanted to write out my thoughts and feelings. I would do this as much to inform them as to console myself.

I grabbed a pen. It felt as if my past had come back to haunt me in more ways than I ever could have imagined. Even though I had tried to set up my adult life for success, I felt that I was now doomed for failure.

I finally put pen to paper and started writing about my life from the beginning. It's funny to think that when I was a child, the worst thing that had happened to me was my parents' divorce. That monumental event had started me on a path of unforgiving resentment. And it impacted my ability to have healthy relationships. That early rupture in our family felt like the root to every problem I faced thereafter.

*   *   *   *   *

1981

Memphis, Tennessee

I can't remember much about the divorce itself. At just four years old, I was too young to understand it and had no idea what was happening, nor could I possibly imagine that this single marital event would change my life in the most profound ways.

As a four-year-old, I thought I had the best parents in the entire world. What other kid in Memphis, Tennessee, could say they got to go to carnivals on a weekly basis *and* were given an unlimited number of balloons to play with? No one could except for me and my older brother, James, who looked just like me, both of us innocent and happy-go-lucky.

Our parents, James and Wanda Braglia, had gotten married in 1975, both of them quite young, my mom eighteen and my dad twenty-four. Together, they owned their own special events business, which sold Mylar balloons, head bobbers, and blow-up plastic toys—perfect for carnivals, parties, and community events. And they advertised their products by dressing up as clowns at the numerous county fairs in our area.

It must have been a successful enough business, as we lived in a spacious, five-bedroom split-level home, complete with an orange-themed living room with felt wallpaper, decor typical of the seventies.

Thinking about those balloons may seem a little silly now. But to kids everywhere, they were helium wonders. We loved holding them in our hands or letting them go and watching them fly above us—floating away into the atmosphere. As a four-year-old, those balloons were symbols of joy—the best life a kid could have!

Like most little kids, I idolized my parents, depended on them, and loved everything about them. My mother looked like a fashion model with long brown hair, a beautiful smile, and a perfect figure. Dad was quite tall and handsome, well-built with thick brown hair and a mustache. They were a striking couple for sure. And in my eyes, they could do no wrong.

My mother was always the calm one in the house, very business-minded, the salesperson in the marital team. She had been working in and out of retail stores and sometimes hosted home parties where she sold sexy lingerie.

On the other hand, my father, raised by his 100 percent Italian family, was quite stubborn and hotheaded, and far more impulsive than my mother. He didn't communicate very well and easily lost his cool, which led him to swearing a lot. My father was a man who didn't offer a lot of compliments. He wasn't a bad person, necessarily, but he didn't know how to communicate, and he lacked skills to nurture or validate any of us with his words. I became aware much later in my own adult life that he parented in the way he had been parented. He modeled what he saw in his own childhood.

One day, we were all getting ready to accompany my parents to a full day at the carnival. My brother, my uncle Marvin, and I were helping get things situated as usual when something out of the ordinary happened—an event that would change our lives forever.

As we arrived at the carnival grounds, there was an exceptionally high feeling of excitement in the air. Though that kind of buzz was common, it seemed especially invigorating on that day.

With the unmistakable smell of popcorn wafting through the air, we threw ourselves into the swirl of all the people laughing and milling around. Children squealed with joy on the amusement rides and young couples held hands as they played games, competing for the giant stuffed panda prizes. To a kid, the carnival was everything it was supposed to be and more.

As always, my brother and I were enjoying the VIP life of carnival kids who got free tickets to all our favorite rides, including Tilt-A-Whirl. We had a blast.

So how could such a wonderful day turn into a life-changing trauma, a day that I would despise for the rest of my life?

That afternoon, after my parents finished working, we all went home. But it wasn't long before they changed clothes and began getting ready to go back out again, this time without me and my brother. They told us that they were leaving to have some alone time and that Uncle Marvin would take care of us.

Much as we loved my mother's brother, he wasn't necessarily our first choice for a babysitter. Uncle Marvin was a fit bachelor who looked a little like Elvis Presley. He was always dating beautiful women and focused on his own personal life. He had no clue about kids and possessed no domestic skills. He didn't even know how an oven worked, much less how to cook a meal, so he made most of his meals in a microwave.

That night, as we were starving for dinner, our parents assured us that our uncle would feed us well. But given his skills, that was questionable. My parents then gave my brother and me tight hugs and kisses, told us they loved us, and left the house.

We turned to watch Uncle Marvin rustling through the refrigerator to find something to make for dinner, and he eventually found a frozen dinner that he could heat up for us.

Meanwhile, my brother and I began to play with the leftover balloons my parents had placed in the living room. After about a half hour, as we pushed the balloons into the air, we began to smell something cooking. Maybe it was because we were so hungry, but the aroma of whatever Uncle Marvin had made was actually quite appealing.

Plates were set on the table and our uncle called us over to eat. It was a frozen veal parmesan, our favorite. My brother and I dug in enthusiastically. But after the first bite, we quickly realized there was something *awful* about this food. The problem was that the dinner had not been cooked all the way through, which meant our uncle couldn't even follow instructions on a frozen food package!

"Yuck! This is nasty!" I yelled as I spit the veal back onto the plate. My reaction pissed off Marvin, and he began to scream at me: "Eat your food!" His harsh tone stung us, and my brother then began to cry.

I was defiant: "I don't want to eat this . . . . It's making my stomach hurt!" Uncle Marvin's anger turned into a look of confusion as he took a bite of the veal. "Oh shit, this *is* nasty!" he agreed. "Come on, we're going out to eat."

My brother and I were only too happy to get our jackets and leave to get some real food. As it turned out, my uncle took us to Burger King, which had a delicious veal parmesan sandwich on its menu. It was our favorite. As we ate together, we all laughed about how nasty the food was that Uncle Marvin had made. Afterward, we were happy to head back home, extremely tired after what had been such a long, happy day.

*   *   *   *   *

We got back home around the same time my parents did, which was a nice surprise since we didn't think we would be seeing them until morning.

At that point, as Uncle Marvin went up to sleep in the spare room, my parents told me and my brother to change into our pajamas and then come in their bedroom. They wanted to talk to us before we went to sleep.

As we both climbed into the bed with them, we could see from their expressions that something was not quite right.

Even at age four, I knew that something bad was happening, and I could do nothing to stop it. There was a tension in the atmosphere that you could cut with a knife.

As my mother spoke, tears began rolling down her cheeks. I understood the emotion, but her words made no sense to me at all. My father then stepped in and explained, "Your mom and I love you both very much. But things are about to change a little. We are going to spend some time apart from each other, which means you and your brother won't see me as much as usual."

He finished by announcing, "We're getting a *divorce*." The mention of that word led both our parents to start crying together. Then James and I began to cry, too, even though we had absolutely no idea what that word *divorce* even meant. None of it made any sense to us. The only thing that was clear was that my father was going to leave the house and that our lives were about to drastically change.

It was a traumatic night, a total blur beginning with the announcement, then the tears, and my own confusion and panic. Children are obviously bonded to their parents, and any change like a temporary separation (much less the threat of a total absence) is life-shattering. My brother and I cried ourselves to sleep that night. And when we woke up the next morning, our father was gone. My stomach was in knots because I instinctively believed that Daddy was never going to come back.

Much later on, as an adult, I found out that my father had been emotionally and verbally abusive to our mom. And she had tolerated it for *five* years. Why? The reasons are not surprising. As a naive girl who had married so young, she didn't know any different. But eventually, as unhappy as she was with Dad, she had an affair. Since my father was her first and only sexual partner, she may have been curious. And she was certainly eager to be with somebody who would treat her better than my father did. It was true that my dad had built her a brand-new house as a wedding gift, and on the surface he treated her well. What she didn't recognize, and neither did we as children, was Dad's explosive temper and cutting remarks had slowly added up, turning into emotional damage for my mother. My dad allowed people to disrepect us and treat us as though we were not good enough. His family treated him this way, and he carried that treatment over to us. We know not what we do.

In any case, her actions precipitated the split. Dad was, of course, both shocked and infuriated by what she had done. And being hotheaded to begin with, there was no way he was going to stay at home to work it out with her. So after my father found out about what she'd done, he didn't fight to stay; he just threw in the towel and left as if we were not worth fighting for. It was the end.

Mom told Dad that she wanted a fast divorce and that he could keep any personal belongings he wanted as long as she had full physical custody of us. She inadvisably agreed that he didn't even have to pay child support. She was only 18 when they got married. There was no way everything was going to be perfect. But I still wonder why he didn't fight for his family, why it was so easy for him to walk away.

My mother agreed to this raw financial deal because she just wanted to keep us in the house with her. And maybe her acquiescence was partly due to her guilt for having an affair in the first place. In any case, the agreement was that Dad would come take us for visits with him every other weekend. And that was it. He got us everything we needed, and we never went without.

*   *   *   *   *

After my father left, Uncle Marvin, who helped run the

balloon business with my mom, moved in with us permanently. The idea was that he would support her around the house while also helping out with paying the bills.

With my father gone, Mom seemed to be doing just fine without him. But it was very sad for me and my brother. We were used to having breakfast with our dad every morning and missed him so much.

Meanwhile, seemingly the next day, my mom's close friend Mindy came to visit us. She was a party girl and really funny, someone my mother enjoyed being around. And Mom needed someone to confide in during this difficult time. It wasn't long before Mom announced that Mindy would *also* be living with us temporarily, until she could find a place to stay of her own. Everything was changing fast.

We now had a new family unit—Mom, Uncle Marvin, my brother, me, and Mindy. Although the house was full, it still felt empty without Dad. Then one day, out of the blue, another guy showed up at our house, who was introduced to us as Mindy's boyfriend, Justin.

Something seemed very odd about him. He was a skinny guy who didn't talk very much. He was quite serious and always depressed. And he was a big drinker, too, which was probably his way of dealing with depression.

Despite his moodiness, it seemed that Justin was way nicer to my mom than he was to his supposed girlfriend, Mindy. Sometimes, it didn't even look to me like Mindy cared about her "boyfriend." It turned out that the explanation of

Justin being Mindy's boyfriend was just a cover. My mother felt it looked bad that she was dating another man so quickly, so she attempted to hide it from us.

But I noticed that Justin would hug and kiss Mom the way Dad used to hug and kiss her. I could see that my mom was happy anytime Justin was close to her, so I was happy for her, too, even though I still missed Dad.

My mom decided that it was time for all of us, including my dad and Mindy's "boyfriend," to move back to Illinois, which was where my parents had grown up and where we were born and had lived for a short time. I don't really remember when my parents uprooted us to Tennessee. Now, we were all planning to move back and start over, whatever that was supposed to mean. Too many things were already uncharted, unknown, and unclear.

CHAPTER TWO

Papa Don't Preach

1983
Crestwood, Illinois

DURING THIS STRANGE overlap of relationships, with my mother separated from my father and now intimately involved with Justin, and all of us moving to Illinois, my whole world seemed unstable. Within months of moving to Illinois, my mother and father officially divorced. Everything seemed like it was happening so fast.

We moved to Crestwood, where my father got a factory job. He had a small apartment just down the street from us and picked us up every other weekend for visitation. He also showed up at every one of our school events, never missing out on anything. James and I always looked forward to those visits with our dad because at home there was Justin. We didn't like him, and we knew he didn't care much for us either.

Justin was down and irritable a lot of the time, filling our house with tension. He always claimed his depression was because he hated Illinois and that my mom "made" him move there to be with her. Justin drank a lot, probably to numb himself, and was often not very nice. It seemed like he hated his life. And I can tell you that he certainly had no interest in being a father figure. We didn't want any relationship with him either, so we stayed as far away as we could.

The only thing we wanted was for our dad to come and get us, to rescue us. When he did come to pick us up, we would do fun things together, like making cinnamon rolls in his kitchen, going to the movies, or just hanging out around the house and talking or watching a favorite movie like John Travolta's *Urban Cowboy*.

These were the kinds of diverting things my mother never had time to do with us anymore. She was so weighed down, trying to raise kids while working long hours in women's retail clothing to make ends meet. Plus, she had to deal with relationship issues with Justin. It wasn't easy for her.

Dad became the "fun" parent. So being with him was just hang-out time. Of course, unlike my mom, he didn't have to deal with homework, getting us to school, or bedtime. But we preferred his company since mom was suffering, clearly not in a happy relationship, and hence more difficult to be with. Things weren't about to get any better.

Soon after arriving in Illinois, my mother sat us down and told us that we were going to be "a big brother and sister"—she was pregnant!

And after that announcement, it seemed like Justin was out all the time, while mom cried a lot at home.

My father had no clue about the pregnancy, though he was soon fully apprised of it. I think he might have been jealous, but he said it didn't bother him at all. Meanwhile, he had a girlfriend, too, so everybody was romantically occupied in our dysfunctional little group.

As for me, though I couldn't fully understand a lot of what was happening, I did grasp some things. My new little baby brother or sister was Justin's child, not my father's.

Although I might have felt angry about this odd family situation as a teenager or young adult, I was still too young to be upset. Nor did I understand how this new baby would affect our family. For a little girl who loved playing with dolls, I was just excited there was going to be a new baby in the house. And I couldn't wait to be a big sister.

Justin, however, didn't seem as excited as everyone else about my mother's pregnancy and the impending arrival of a baby. In fact, he never seemed to be very thrilled about *anything*. He continued to be grouchy and moody. He almost never said anything nice to me or to my brother or to any other kids who came over to play with us. Justin made me believe that he didn't like me or my brother and that he wasn't going to like our new baby brother or sister either. The more unhappy he seemed about the baby, the more my mom toiled with her unstable emotions.

My mother was immensely overwhelmed, which to

James and me looked like unhappiness and filled our house with sorrow. How could she still want to be with a man who made her cry all the time? I just didn't get it.

One day when my dad dropped me and my brother off after our visit, he came inside to find my mom alone and crying. He went over to her and asked her what was wrong, while my brother and I just stood there, wondering the same thing.

My mother told me and James to go to our rooms so that she could finish talking to Dad alone. We left the room but made sure to peek around the corner and try to hear what was being said. We couldn't really make out the specifics, but we saw our mother break down in tears. And then our father comforted her by giving her the tightest hug and whispering in her ear.

This sign of affection was all my brother and I needed to give us hope that Justin would leave one day and our dad would come back home again. From that moment on, for every birthday I had, my only wish was that my parents would get back together again. That was all I wanted, and it was all I needed.

That day when Mom was so upset, as we watched our parents talk for what seemed like forever, our hopes grew that he wouldn't leave at all. Unfortunately, that moment was short-lived, and our dad drove away.

And regrettably, Justin came back into the house. A little while later he was having yet another fight with our mom. I felt helpless over the situation. It was miserable for everybody, hardly the life my mother had hoped for.

If I had known what depression was, I would have thought that I was for sure. But as a five-year-old, I couldn't possibly absorb the meaning of what was happening all around me, even though it was victimizing me and my brother.

How could Mom not see what we wanted, which was for our dad to come back home again? Did she even care how we felt?

More to the point, did she care about herself?

*   *   *   *   *

As time passed, with Dad paying no child support and Justin drifting from one low-paying job to another, we were forced to downsize on everything. The stress on Mom must have been incredible. It's painful for a child to see a parent continually upset. And I remember seeing my mother cry constantly.

Many childhood memories that are fuzzy on facts remain emotionally distinct. I understood that my mother was now in a compromised situation—living with an unpleasant man who was abusive, and supporting herself on far less than what she had earned when she owned the balloon business with Dad. That euphoric time of life was now just a distant memory as Mom's stomach got bigger and bigger.

Before we knew it, my family was downsizing into a two-bedroom apartment located in Tinley Park, a suburb southwest of Chicago. My brother and I had to share a bedroom. This place was much smaller than the one we used to live in, but it was all my mother could afford.

As though money issues and the pregnancy weren't enough reasons to be worried and stressed, she was constantly dealing with Justin. As far as I could see, he was the real reason for her despair.

I began to hate him. As I've mentioned, he would yell at my mom frequently and reduce her to sobs by saying the meanest things. Ever since Justin entered the picture, the only thing I could see was Mom constantly trying to hold it together and fake her happiness. You could tell by the way she'd suddenly start smiling when we came into the room, while her eyes convyed sadness. We could tell when she had been crying; she couldn't mask that with a flimsy upward turn of her lips.

With our family finances strapped, Justin luckily got a new job, but it was in Romeoville, a tiny town southwest of Chicago near Interstate 55. So we had to move yet again. They found a three-bedroom house, but it was still cramped which made things even more miserable. The fights between my mother and Justin were even worse than before. She would beg him to stay home and not go out again; he would tell her to shut up and mind her own business and that she didn't own him. Even when they weren't fighting, you could feel the tension in the house.

I sometimes wondered if they had argued this much

before and we just hadn't heard them. But now we could hear them loud and clear.

My brother and I were huddled together like prisoners, praying for my dad to return home and save us, as if he were a knight in shining armor. Although it is many divorced child's dream to have their parents reunite, that dream totally dissipated with the birth of my baby sister, Melissa. With her birth, I felt as if there was no hope that our father would ever return.

Of course, he wasn't going to return anyway.

*   *   *   *   *

When we relocated to Romeoville, my mother decided to send me and my brother to a Catholic school for the remainder of our elementary education. This new school was much more advanced than the regular public schools we were accustomed to. The homework had been easy for us then, but now, just keeping up with the assignments became difficult. In fact, James and I began to fail in every subject area.

Due to our poor performance, the school decided that we were not ready to advance to our proper grade levels (third for me, fourth for my brother) when it came to certain subjects like cursive, so we were both placed in the *first* grade classroom for a couple of hours each day so that we could begin to catch up with our classmates. Being bumped out of our class for even a couple of hours made us feel stupid, like losers. Being the new kids in class didn't help us either. We were outsiders, displaced from the friends we had just begun to make in our previous school. But we didn't want to ask anyone for help. My mother noticed we were struggling, and she realized that if we didn't get it together, the school was going to fail us. She preempted that possibility by pulling us out of the school to spare us any more embarrassment.

One day after coming home from our new school, my mother said she wanted to speak with me and James. That night at the dinner table, she announced that we would now be moving to a public school in Romeoville. I think she thought this would make us happy. James and I did *not* mind to move to another school because we hated wearing uniforms and our grades were failing. However, we did not want to lose the few new friends we had already made.

That night, Mom made sure to tell us, "Eat your vegetables! They're getting cold." She warned us that if we didn't eat our vegetables, we would sit at the table all night until we finished them. James and I used to think that if we fought Mom on certain issues, she would eventually give in, but that was not the case this time. She made us sit at the table for what seemed like days until we finally finished those nasty carrots. Eventually, our dog, Buster, a chocolate lab, came in from outside and scooted under the kitchen table. Of course, my brother and I fed *him* the vegetables! Why not?

The phone rang and my mother went to answer it. Perhaps because of our turbulent homelife, James and I had become extremely nosy kids. We always wanted to be "in the know." So, of course, we tried to eavesdrop on our mother's conversation. We couldn't hear what the person on the other end was saying, but we could hear Mom's end of the call. She looked nervous and scared.

"Hello? What kind of underwear am I wearing? *Who is this?*"

As my mother turned to catch me and my brother listening to her conversation, she quickly hung up the phone. But as soon as she did, the phone started to ring again.

"Stop calling my house!" she yelled as she hung up the phone for a second time. James and I weren't actually scared until after the second time Mom hung up. That's when she started looking through the blinds to see if anyone was outside; she next checked the doors to make sure they were all locked.

Clearly, Mom was terrified, with nobody there to protect her. As always, Justin was absent; he seemed to spend all his free time at the bar. No doubt, his drinking contributed to his unpredictable behavior toward our mom.

*   *   *   *   *

1987
Romeoville, Illinois

By the time my stepsister, Melissa, was four years old and I was nine, we had a new addition to our family, a baby sister named Drew Ann. Melissa started sharing a room with me and my brother when we moved to Romeoville. Our room was a menagerie, filled with tons of stuffed animals spread all over our beds and the floor. We spent hours playing together, and I must say that I liked having younger sisters.

But what I didn't like was waking up every morning soaking wet because Melissa, who was being potty-trained, would pee all over me during the night. (We nicknamed her Melissa Pissa.) I remember getting so mad and screaming at my mother to get Melissa Pissa her *own* bed because I was sick and tired of waking up with my side of the bed soaked and then having to clean it all by myself. Naturally, because I was older, it was expected that I would clean up after my younger sister.

Despite the tiny house and cramped quarters, and even despite Justin and Mom's ups and downs, I felt normalcy and happiness here. As an adult healing from the trauma of my childhood, I now know that this was the time and place when I felt happiest and safest as a child. And when things felt chaotic or unstable at times, I escaped in music—listening to songs intended for much older children, like Madonna's "Papa Don't Preach," which was one of my favorites. I certainly felt as if I had grown up rather quickly, not a baby anymore for sure.

*   *   *   *   *

One morning close to Christmas, as I was getting ready for school, my mother told me that our regular babysitter, Stacy, was going to come and watch us after school. "So you be on your best behavior," she told me.

I went straight home after school and was about to pull out my keys to enter from the back door, but it was wide open. That seemed strange. I walked in intending to ask who had left the door open, but when I got inside, the house was completely empty, not a sound to be heard. My sisters and James hadn't made it back from school yet. I was the first to arrive. Where was Stacy?

What I saw next scared the hell out of me. In my bedroom, there was writing all over the wall. Somebody had used a dark, blood-red color and smeared the letters together in a way that was difficult for me to read. I was only eight and still learning to read, but I could definitely decipher one word that made me frantic: *Die.*

I felt panicked and had no idea what to do. All I knew was that I was home alone, and my babysitter was not there. I did the only thing I could think of and called my mother at work, a women's retail store at the mall. As I ran past the bathroom to get the phone, I noticed writing in there as well. Scribbles of the same red color with a little bit of black mixed into the letters was smeared on the bathroom mirror: *I'm going to kill you.*

Honestly, at this point, I stood frozen in fear, just taking it all in. I then ran out of the bathroom and stumbled into the living room where the house phone was on the hook. My hands were shaking as I tried to dial my mother's work phone. Meanwhile, I was trying to keep a lookout for the intruder, who might still be in the house.

After the third ring, someone answered, and I urgently asked to speak to my mother. She came right away. And just as I heard her voice, the tears I had been trying to hold back started to stream down my face. "Mom!" I screamed. "Oh my God, Mom! I came home and the back door was open and there is writing all over the house and somebody is trying to kill me, and Stacy is not here, and I'm scared!"

I realized that after spouting all of that off without pausing for a breath, my mother may not have understood a word. She told me, "Just calm down, let me see if I can find out where Stacy is, okay?"

As soon as I had hung up the phone, I heard three knocks on the door. It was Stacy, and I could not have been more elated.

"Stacy! Oh my God, Stacy, I am so happy you are here!" I shouted. "Look! Somebody wrote all over the walls and in the bathroom and my room too! I'm scared . . . What do we do?!"

But Stacy looked very calm and said, "Don't worry, everything is going to be okay. I'm going to call your mom so we can see what we need to do."

As Stacy picked up the phone, a huge wave of relief washed over me. Just having Stacy in the house immediately calmed me down. I watched her as she talked to my mom, but I wasn't really hearing anything because my mind was still wrapped around the fact that someone had broken into our house. I couldn't shake off the uneasy feeling.

My mother told Stacy to look around the house in every closet and corner to make sure that there wasn't anyone hiding there and to assess if they had taken anything. So Stacy grabbed my hand and, together, we walked around the house to inspect what damage had been done.

The house was in complete disarray: There was crystal broken all over the floor behind the bar; a pie had been thrown into the popcorn maker; the waterbed was leaking because someone had stabbed holes in it. Not to mention furniture toppled over and paperwork thrown all over the floor. I just couldn't wrap my mind around what had actually happened in our home. And from this point forward, I was afraid to be alone at all. Stacy continued to assure me that everything was going to be okay and did everything she could to calm me down.

Later that day, when my mother came home, she realized that there were some items missing from the house, including Justin's Walkman. When she realized it was gone, a determined and suspicious look came over her face that I had never seen before.

The next morning, Mom was on the phone, calling Stacy's high school and asking the principal to search Stacy's locker. A few hours later, I found out that the missing Walkman was found inside Stacy's locker. Needless to say, Stacy didn't babysit for us after that day.

Despite the Walkman being found in Stacy's possession, she swore she wasn't the person who had vandalized our house. And despite her dishonesty (and thievery), they believed her. That left only one person to blame. The only other person who had been there to discover it all—me.

As soon as I walked in from school that day, my mother was at the door screaming at me, hurling an absurd accusation: "Why did you write all over the walls in the house and the bathroom?! What were you *thinking?*" I was in total shock as she hollered at me for at least twenty minutes, blaming me for all the damage that was done to the house during the break-in the day before.

How could she think that I was responsible for the writing on the walls? I was just a kid and obviously had nothing to do with it. Where would an eight-year-old get fake blood or real blood? How could an eight-year-old cause that much damage? Of course, I tried to tell my mom that, swearing up and down that it wasn't true, but she just wouldn't listen or believe me. Instead, she punished me by grounding me for a week.

At this point, I could not hold back the tears or the pain. The sense of betrayal I felt from my mother was a stain on my soul that I would never let go of or forget. As I ran into my room and closed the door, I was thinking, *How could my own mother not believe me? Why would I destroy my own house? More importantly, why would she believe that I would do this? Am I that bad of a kid that she thinks such horrible things of me?*

As I slammed the door, I could hear my mother charging into the room after me. "You slam that damn door one more time, you will be grounded for the entire month!" I seriously could not believe this was happening to me, and all I could do was cry into my pillow.

The next morning, I woke up on the soggiest pillow imaginable, as I had cried myself to sleep. But the entire mood of the house had now shifted. I could hear my mom and stepdad and our neighbors talking and laughing loudly outside my door. They were drinking together and having a grand old time. Meanwhile, I was still hurt by the fact that my mom thought I destroyed our house; but now I was even more upset that she was having such a good time while I was still upset and grounded.

As it turned out, it was our neighbor next door, the one who often flirted with my mom, who had broken into our house. He was also the person who had called and inquired about the underwear my mother was wearing. We just didn't know about it until the day before we moved out of that house when he told my mom.

Here I was, grounded for my alleged vandalism and theft of our own home. I wasn't to leave my room or go anywhere. I eventually fell back asleep and woke up the next morning to my family pulling out the Christmas decorations. It was always a festive time around our house during the holidays, and decorating the Christmas tree was one of our favorite events to do together as a family.

For some reason, it was not as festive in the house as I would have hoped. The mood had shifted yet again in a more ominous direction. That was the thing about our house. Up until this instance, we had loved living here. We would be outside playing with our friends from sun up to sun down. It was the time of our life.

My mother and Justin were arguing because Justin wanted to go out with his drinking buddies instead of putting up the tree with his family. My mother was telling him that he *couldn't* go out, so he started yelling at her even louder. The next thing I knew, Justin had gotten up and pushed my mother so hard that she fell right into the Christmas tree. Of course, we knew that Justin could be mean, and he was always yelling at our mother. But we had never seen him be so physical with her before, even if I suspected it was happening behind closed doors. The anger I felt watching this man shove my mother with such force was immense. But I was young and felt utterly helpless; I could not do anything about it.

My mother fell over with the Christmas tree and I heard the loudest crack ever, which was the sound of the tree stand breaking into two parts. All this happened so quickly that we just stood there, shocked at how the holiday mood in the house had deteriorated into this horror. Next thing I knew, my mother was telling us to go straight to our rooms—no questions asked—so we dutifully did so, but not before stopping to look around the corner to see what happened.

There was more arguing. Although it was inaudible, we

got the gist of it. My mother was telling Justin that he had to leave the house and *not come back*. But it didn't look like he was going to leave on his own anytime soon. My mother picked up the phone, and within minutes police officers were at our door. Although we couldn't hear what was going on, we watched as the police walked Justin out of the house.

Finally, it seemed that our mother was choosing herself and us. I was so relieved to have him escorted away that I nearly forgave her for not believing me and banishing me to my room the day before. Perhaps now with Justin gone she would start to listen and pay attention to us again. We were certain that was the end of him, and I was certain I might have a chance at getting my mom back. Or so I hoped.

CHAPTER THREE

The Decision

1988
Romeoville, Illinois

A FEW WEEKS after Justin was escorted from our house by police, my mother sat me and James down in our living room and told us that she had to speak with us. Anytime she brought us into a room and told us this, we dreaded what she would say. Because whatever it was it was usually nothing good.

But on this occasion, we were shocked to discover we were being forced to make a decision that would turn out to be detrimental to our well-being. My mother announced that she was moving back to Tennessee with Justin to appease him. She thought doing so would allow him to be a better person as he was always blaming his mood and failures on having moved away. And she wanted to know if we wanted to move back with her or stay in Illinois and live with our dad.

Imagine your own mother telling you that she's leaving with or without you.

I understood what she was asking us, but I was distracted by her own poor judgment. I just couldn't believe that she would want to live with this man in a relationship that I saw as toxic and abusive. But as I would learn later in life, victims often stay with their abusers due to fear of being alone, low self-esteem, lack of financial means, or fear that the abuser's actions will become more violent and maybe even lethal if the victim attempts to leave. They can become addicted to the cycles of abuse. Or it can be any combination of these reasons why victims stay.

In my mother's case, I believe because she felt she let her first marriage end without a fight, she didn't want it to happen a second time. She thought she should give it her all and had to keep it together. In truth, I think she believed that we would be better off with our dad, who would protect us from her toxic relationship with Justin. Although she was very upset about the prospect of leaving, I think she also felt a sense of relief.

As an eleven-year-old child, of course, I could not grasp the complex reason for my mother's poor decision-making. But more importantly, I knew for sure that I did *not* want to stick around to watch anymore. My brother made the decision first and said he was going to live with our dad. I agreed I was going to stay with them too. So a few days later we told Mom that we had decided to stay with our dad in Illinois. It was a hard decision that no child should have to make. And

I don't think we really understood the choice that we were faced with.

Yes, we loved our dad and wanted to be with him. But we also loved our mom and did not want to be separated from her. Plus, there was another wrenching part to the decision. We were going to lose our two younger sisters, Melissa and Drew Ann, as Justin was their father and obviously taking them with him to Tennessee.

To say the least, losing our mom and sisters was traumatic for me and James. We would now be alone with just Dad. But despite the obvious sacrifices, the thought of living in the same house with Justin was horrible. So we stuck to our decision that living with our dad was where we wanted to be.

When moving day came at the end of summer, I realized that nothing in my life would ever be the same again. All I remember were the tears. It was the most sorrowful afternoon as my mom hugged both me and my brother tightly, the three of us crying together. The family as we had known it all our lives was gone, and part of me second-guessed my decision. I honestly didn't know whether we had made the right decision or not. Maybe this was the worst mistake I would ever make.

All I knew in that moment was that I desperately needed my mom. For a long time, I felt she had abandoned us for a man who was undeserving of her. I couldn't see that she was caught between a rock and a hard place, desperately wanting this second marriage to work but at the cost of her two older children.

Why, I thought, *would she leave the state just to accommodate Justin's desire to move?* I couldn't understand why any woman would ever leave her children for such a toxic relationship. But it was her choice to leave—and her choice to leave us behind.

So that day, I stood there clinging to my mother, a sixth grader losing so much of her family. After the emotional goodbyes, my dad drove me and my brother to our new home—a two-bedroom apartment in Orland Park, a much higher-end neighborhood from where we had been living. Because I was the only girl in the house, I got a room to myself, while my father and brother shared.

I can still remember that first night in my new room; I cried for hours until I finally fell asleep. As a young girl, I had no idea how to handle my grief and the intense separation anxiety I was feeling. Remember, this was before FaceTime or Zoom, so Mom being in another state was especially hard. It was just the most horrible feeling being in that new bedroom all alone, missing my mom and my sister, who was my roommate. I was a mess, and I couldn't do anything to fix it. For the next days, *nothing* made me happy. My father tried to keep us busy and engaged, buying new things for the apartment and getting school supplies. But I was despondent, feeling as if I had lost control of my life.

After a while, I began to adjust and got into the new routine of living with my dad. Since he was always gone before we woke up, we would get ready for school on our own. We'd make our own breakfast and pack a lunch before we got on the bus.

As for the atmosphere at home, without my two little sisters to play with, I felt a little lost and quite alone. It was so quiet! No longer was there anybody to clean up after or laugh with or play with outside.

From my brother's perspective, he actually liked being with my dad full time. You might say that our father was a "weekend" dad. His sole focus was using his off time to have fun with us. But there was more to the job of being a dad, and prior to our moving in with him, he had never been the one helping with our homework and feeding us dinner.

Much as I appreciated his efforts, there were some things that a dad could never do. For example, as a girl entering puberty with no mother to advise me, I now had to cope with issues like getting my period, shaving my legs, experimenting with makeup, wearing a bra, and having feelings about boys. These were all the kinds of things that I needed a mother for, but she just wasn't there.

Of course, my dad tried to help where he could. But it was so awkward talking to him about the changes in my body that I would often just avoid it share nothing with him at all.

As for our basic needs, Dad always made sure we were taken care of. But his work schedule, a twelve-hour shift from 4:00 a.m. to 4:00 p.m., didn't allow for a lot of one-on-one personal time with him. He was the manager at a breading plant in Melrose Park called Golden Dipt, a company that made pancake batter and the seasoning for breading on chicken and fish.

By the time he got home from such a labor-intensive day, he was always exhausted, certainly too tired to help with homework. However, he always made dinner for us, and together we cleaned up. After dinner, he collapsed in front of the television to watch sports and would fall asleep. So when I needed to talk, he really wasn't emotionally available. But it didn't impact my academic performance at all—at least not yet. What did enter my mind was whether my dad knew how to communicate.

*   *   *   *   *

1991
Orland Park, Illinois

Up until eighth grade, I was an honor roll student and active on the cheerleading poms team, happy to be in a regular, stable routine that distracted me from the loss of my mother. Like any teenage girl, I started to confide more and more in my new friends at school. I was not particularly popular, though I did make some strong friendships. But my school was also filled with a lot of stuck-up people who thought they were better than everyone else. By the time I reached high school, the anger I felt inside toward those who discriminated against others surfaced. And let's just say that nobody messed with me.

My very best friend was a Hispanic girl named Isabel. She was very beautiful with long, black wavy hair. Isabel was the best dancer in the school and was an incredible singer, too, blessed with a beautiful voice. Added to her gifts was her strength; she was tough. Isabel would soon have a huge impact on me.

*   *   *   *   *

Even though I was settling into my new lifestyle, occupied by school and friends, I was still unhappy at home. My father had a hair-trigger temper and swore at us a lot when he was mad about *anything*.

As kids, if we accidently dropped or broke a glass, he went ballistic: "Goddamn you, motherfuckers!" he would yell as if I had dropped the glass on purpose. So used to his flared temper and outbursts, I grew to have no fear.

Decades later, as I began to do personal development work, I learned that living in this kind of tense atmosphere is very traumatic to any child. It's likely the reason I ran from home as much as I could, escaping his emotional and verbal abuse that was destroying me from the inside out. As a teenager, however, I didn't know I was experiencing emotional abuse or trauma and I certainly didn't know how to talk about what I was feeling.

On one level, I know Dad did his best and that he loved me. But his "best" was not good enough. And love is no license for mistreating us. It wasn't until years later that I began to understand how the cycle of emotional abuse can be perpetuated through a child's entire life. Only the strongest do the work to heal from that abuse and break the cycle so it does not continue for generations to come.

There I was, a teenager going through the usual angst of adolescence while coping with my father's temper and separation anxiety from Mom. In the back of my mind, I was always remembering the friction and stress in the household that we had left and the one that we were in now. Emotional abuse is silent but deadly. Inside your body, it knows its wrong, but your brain doesn't catch up until you start doing the work to heal or find harmful ways to cope. My friends showed me all the wrong ways of coping—mostly by drinking beer and getting high.

I can't blame the start of my drug use on my father or mother. But Mom's absence certainly didn't help. And Dad's behavior was unacceptable. Ultimately, my substance use was a way to escape reality. I began to self-destruct because I didn't feel worthy or loved.

So during the summer of eighth grade, I started drinking and smoking weed, enabled by Isabel's brother and friends who had access to drugs. The first time I got high was an incredible escape from my reality. Drinking made me feel better instantly, allowing me to escape whatever I was feeling but unable to express.

I realize now that I gravitated toward self-destructive

behaviors because I didn't feel like anyone really cared about me. If no one cared about me, then it didn't matter what they said about my behavior. If no one cared about me, maybe I didn't care about myself either. Substance abuse was also a response to feeling both ignored and like I wasn't as good as others—a horrible state of mind that left me feeling incredibly empty.

I don't think I ever got over my parents' split or the instability it created, with my mother in one state and an absentee father in another. But on drugs, I was launched into a relaxed, euphoric state of mind that allowed me to forget my real life. What a relief.

I now had more freedom than any teenager should ever be allowed to have. It was the perfect storm: My mom was no longer there to provide discipline and structure, and my dad was completely tuned out, exhausted from work and inattentive about everything. I had free rein and felt as if I could do *anything* I wanted to do.

So if I wanted to go and hang out with Isabel or any of my other friends all night long, I just left the house. Being with Isabel helped me forget how lonely I felt.

As time passed, Isabel and I became inseparable. As I look back on it now, I don't want to say that she was a bad influence, but she did fuel the fire of my rebellion. I would always sleep over at her house and we would sneak out or drink without anyone knowing about it. She was all about taking risks—sex with new boys, trying out combinations of alcohol and drugs, whatever she could do. And during this period of my life, I began experimenting with these things too.

One time I stayed over at Isabel's house while her parents were hosting a birthday barbecue for Isabel's brother. As usual, we snuck booze out of the bar, and nobody knew that we were drinking as much as we possibly could.

In fact, that night, we guzzled down so much beer that we memorized the Surgeon General's warning on the side of the beer can!

I felt completely relieved of any and all of my feelings; I was anesthetized by the alcohol. This is how addiction always starts, seductively lulling you into believing that your problems disappear when you're intoxicated (or high, as I learned with marijuana). Who knew drinking beer could make the pain go away so completely? But it did. (Maybe that's why Justin always drank so much, because he was in pain, too, and it allowed him to escape it.)

Once we got to Isabel's room that night of the beer binge, we literally passed out in her bed. We were so drunk we immediately fell into a deep sleep.

Later that morning, after our headaches began to fade, Isabel came up with a plan for the day. She always had a plan. Today it included sneaking out of the house to go and visit her boyfriend—someone who, by law, was too old to be involved with a minor. In order to make our escape, Isabel came up with an ingenious plan: she told me that she once saw a movie in which a girl ties a few bedsheets together to sneak out of her bedroom, and that's exactly what we were going to do.

It might seem insane that we did this, but I went along for the ride because it was an adventure designed so thirteen-year-old Isabel could hook up with an eighteen-year-old guy. I didn't question it at all. Isabel actually had ten bedsheets ready to be knotted together for us to use as a rope to climb out of her bedroom window. She had thought this through. And when we got to the ground, I felt exhilarated, ready to do it again!

We then headed down the block, and at the sight of the guy waiting for her at the corner, Isabel broke into a fast sprint and jumped ecstatically into his arms. As I stood there awkwardly watching, they began a heavy make out session that made me blush.

After their passionate embrace, the guy suggested that we all head over to one of his friend's houses nearby. When we got there and the door opened, I felt a tingle go down my spine as the pungent aroma of marijuana hit me. I had no idea where this night was heading, but I was a little nervous to be in a strange house with four older guys, ages ranging from eighteen to twenty-two.

After we walked in, Isabel's boyfriend introduced me to one of his male friends and quickly disappeared upstairs with Isabel (no doubt to hook up). I was left alone with this guy. As I sat down, he took a huge puff of a homemade joint and passed it over to me. I didn't want to offend him, so I took it, put it to my lips, and inhaled as hard as he did. The sharp inhale resulted in me choking, and I felt embarrassed that I was gagging in front of this guy who was a stranger to me.

He just chuckled and told me to take another hit. "But this time, don't pull too hard," he said. After only the second puff, I felt euphoric. A strange sense of calm washed over my entire being. I remember sitting in the chair looking straight up at the ceiling as if I didn't have a care in the world. Then, suddenly, I felt the warmth of this guy's breath on my neck as he reached over and started kissing me on the mouth. I had never felt so uncomfortable in my entire life. The kissing felt forced, which made me feel trapped and manipulated.

Yet, as an inexperienced teenage girl, I felt powerless, even worried about offending him. Instead of pushing him away, I started to kiss him back even though I didn't want to. After he realized that I would go along with his advances, he tried to take things even further.

As he was aggressively kissing me, I felt his hand slide up my shirt and then slowly move down toward my pants. That is when I put a stop to everything. I smacked his hand away from my thigh and literally jumped out of the chair and went screaming through the house looking for Isabel.

I rushed up the stairs, found a door that was locked, and started banging on it: "Isabel! Let's go now!" She came to the door a mess, her hair all over the place. She looked at my face and didn't even have to ask me if was everything okay. She just knew it was time to go. She said goodbye to her boyfriend, and we rushed out, returning to her house. I was fortunate to have escaped unwanted advances this time.

CHAPTER FOUR

Free-for-All at the Lock-In

1993
Orland Park, Illinois

AS A NAIVE FRESHMAN in high school who knew nothing about boys, I continued to be in awe of Isabel's boldness. To me, she was literally one of the bravest people I ever met. She wasn't afraid to go up to guys at school—or anywhere, for that matter—and skillfully flirt with them, letting them know that she liked them and that she was available.

She didn't hesitate to get close to them in a sexual way, too, which was the complete opposite of my MO Being around guys that I liked made me nervous and withdrawn. I knew that if they liked me back, they would expect me to immediately start a physical relationship, which made me even more apprehensive. I was still quite shy, obviously a virgin, and not as ready as Isabel to throw myself into a boy's arms, or at least I didn't think I was.

Although I wasn't as bold as Isabel, I still had my crushes, including a huge one on Isabel's friend Luis, a short, very cute Hispanic guy with chubby cheeks who was a year older than me. Every time he came around, I got all giddy. And eventually, as he started being more friendly, I began to think that it was because he had a crush on me too.

One weekend, I went with a group of girls from high school to go hang out at our local roller rink, one of the best around because it had a DJ in the booth who took song requests from kids down on the skate floor. This rink was Isabel's "spot," her favorite hangout place, a showcase for her. She was both an agile skater and a great dancer. And nobody I knew could skate as well as she could.

When we got to the rink that night, Luis was there with his friend Chris, someone else that Isabel had a crush on. And she was there to impress. As Isabel did her thing down on the skate floor, you could see everyone gathering in a circle around the rink to watch.

Carol, another friend from school, had also joined the crowd to watch Isabel busting a move. Carol and I had originally met in the sixth grade, but we grew closer as we entered high school. Standing in the circle watching Isabel was when I first noticed a boy named Logan, who was across the way on the other side of the circle of admirers. He was just as good a skater as Isabel and quite handsome, as was his cousin Kirk. But Luis pulled my attention away, coming up to stand next to me.

As Luis and I got a little closer, he asked if I wanted

a piece of gum, When I said yes, he opened it, put it in his mouth, and told me to come and get it! I did just that. Before I knew it, we were kissing.

Unlike that forced kiss at the party, this was exciting and much less uncomfortable. I guess it was because I wanted Luis to like me as much as I liked him. In this kiss, I felt a delighted warmth, at ease with a new level of closeness I had never felt before. I had no idea that romantic feelings for a guy could be so calming—and so exciting. I loved it. Maybe it was yet another drug. And for the first time, I actually felt comfortable with being sexual.

The roller rink became our new favorite go-to spot to meet up and hang out with everyone. It was the place to be, like a sanctuary, the perfect spot for us to socialize.

One of the best times to be at the rink was during the so-called lock-ins, when only a limited number of skaters were allowed in, after which the doors were locked until sunrise. The rink would be secluded, and nobody would leave until they unlocked the doors at 7 am. It was like a private skate.

Once we were inside, we adopted the "what happens in the rink, stays in the rink" mentality. We could get away with whatever it was we wanted to do at the rink during the lock-ins, which is why so many wild things happened then.

Isabel was now dating one of Luis's friends named Chris, and I was with Luis. Together, we started getting more and more adventurous during these lock-ins. In fact, we started bringing in alcohol and pot every time we met up there.

Drinking and smoking was the norm for us, and we would get quite stoned.

Our lack of inhibitions soon led to all kinds of scenarios. Everywhere you looked, couples were making out. And half the time, the people barely knew each other. I became very comfortable with these make out scenes at the lock-ins, joining in with the rest of the girls. I no longer had any issues with a handsome guy kissing me. In all honesty, I'm surprised the rink was allowed to get away with holding these lock-ins since the teenagers were all out of control—smoking, drinking, and having sex on the premises.

One night after one of these free-for-alls at the rink, Isabel and I went back to Luis's house to continue our "make out party" because we just didn't want to go back to our homes.

As I remember it, Isabel and Chris were going at it hard in the living room, so Luis and I decided to sneak off to get our own privacy. I have no idea how we wound up in the bathroom, but we did. And as soon as we closed the door, Luis began to unbutton my pants and slide his hand down into my panties. I felt his fingers go deep into me. And at that point, I knew we were about to go as far as we could go—all the way. Was I really ready to do this? Was Luis the one?

At the moment I was about to pull Luis's hand away, I felt my pants being slid to the ground, leaving me naked from the waist down. At this point, Luis was ready to penetrate me and guided me down to the floor. He spread my legs open, got in between my thighs, and thrust in for the first of many painful thrusts.

Tears started to roll down my face from the pain of what was happening to me on the bathroom floor. I cringed during every one of Luis's thrusts, in part because of the sounds he was making, as if he was trying to hurt me.

I thought to myself, *Is this what sex is all about? Am I going to have to endure this torture in order for someone to really love me?* There was nothing I enjoyed about the pain I was experiencing, and I laid on that cold floor for what seemed like forever. I just wanted the agony of intercourse to be over. And just when I thought I would have to somehow end this bathroom encounter, Luis groaned in release and then stopped.

He quickly got up from the floor as if he had been relieved of something I didn't know he was carrying. As he pulled up his pants, I wiped the tears from my eyes and stood up, weak-kneed. Then I got dressed. I was in total shock and had no idea what to think about what had just happened.

For some reason, I only wanted to know if Luis was happy. As for me, I didn't know how to process it. I kept asking myself, *What just happened?*

* * * * *

Back at home, my father would have gone ballistic if he knew half of what I was doing, much less having sex on a bathroom floor.

But he finally did start noticing less-than-desirable changes in my behavior, both at home and in school. I honestly couldn't understand how he detected anything about me since he was always at work. To his credit, he became aware and was disturbed by my teenage antics.

The most obvious indicator of my rogue and rebellious behavior was that Luis and I had had sex. When Dad found out, he tried to ground me, telling me that I was no longer allowed to go out with my friends *anywhere*. Since I was used to total independence, I was boiling mad. This argument became the first of many fights to follow with my dad.

In my teenage mind, there was no way he was going to tell me that I couldn't go out with my friends, much less keep me away from my two best friends, Luis and Isabel. After all, they were the only two people who were *there* for me.

Of course, in hindsight, I recognize that Luis wasn't at all good for me. He was not supportive, and he was always fooling around with other people. Yet he was someone who made me feel loved at a time when I was looking for that. I saw in Luis what I wanted to see. Luis was only the first of many relationships that were all the same—empty and void of true love, respect, or companionship.

That evening of the fight, I was supposed to spend the night at Isabel's house, as we already had plans to meet up with Luis and Chris. But my father was not having it. He not only insisted that I could not go out; I couldn't stay over at Isabel's house anymore at all.

In that moment, I decided that my father was not going to tell me what I could or could not do. I told him that I was going out and that there was nothing he could do to stop me. I screamed this at the top of my lungs, then grabbed my coat and walked out of the house. As I hurried down the street, I didn't cry a single tear. I was totally pissed and couldn't believe that my father was suddenly acting like a parent, providing boundaries by forbidding me to leave the house. And in that moment, I started to see that my rage was very similar to his. They say that our greatest relationships are mirrors. The truth is, I was giving him what he was giving me.

As I walked off the anger, I went quite far. And by the time I calmed down, I realized I was halfway to Isabel's house. As I continued along the street, I noticed that a car was trailing me. For a second, I was nervous about my safety, trying to figure out if I might be in line to get kidnapped. But as I turned my head to make eye contact with the driver, I realized it was my dad. And that is when the tears started to pour out of my eyes.

As evil as I was to my father, he had still gotten into his car and followed me halfway across town to make sure that I was okay. As I opened his passenger side door, I bawled and begged at the same time, pleading with him to buy me a pack of cigarettes so that I could calm down, as smoking was also one of my new vices.

He didn't say anything judgmental to me at all. He just pulled over at a gas station, went in and bought me a pack of smokes, and then drove me the rest of the way to Isabel's house. I felt bad—really bad. In his own weird way of enabling me to break his rules, my dad was trying to be a good dad. But there I was giving him hell to pay for everything I had been through, which wasn't entirely his fault.

When I got to Isabels house, everyone was getting ready to go to her cousin's birthday party at Haunted Trails, an outdoor arcade set up on the perimeter of some seasonal haunted houses. As always, Luis was supposed to meet me there. I was especially looking forward to being with him after all the drama I had already been through with my dad. It's amazing how tears can quickly disappear with a rapid change of scene.

As soon as I walked through the door of Haunted Trails and made eye contact with Luis and his friend Drake, I felt the biggest smile appear on my face. This was certainly a day I needed him to cheer me up. I walked right over to Luis, put my hands around his neck and started kissing him like no one else was in the room. Then I took his hand and walked him over to where everyone else was by the Skee-Ball machine. Isabel handed me some tokens and challenged me to a game. I was only too happy to accept as I was somewhat of a Skee-Ball expert.

Isabel and I started a fierce round of the game. During one of my throws, I suddenly felt someone grab my ass. Assuming it was Luis, I turned around with a playful smile on my face. Yet Drake was closer to me. I was pissed, thinking it was Drake.

I gave Drake a death stare, at which point Luis jumped in and tried to say he was actually the one who grabbed me, not Drake. I didn't know who to believe, but I didn't like feeling like a plaything. I turned back around to finish my game with Isabel, who by this point had already beat me by four hundred points.

As I picked up the next ball to throw down the lane, my mind was racing: *Is Luis lying? Did he let Drake do it just to see how I'd respond?* I didn't know what to think, so I just tried to stop thinking about it.

Later that night, my naive teenage world was turned upside down when some girl hanging at the arcade who knew Luis told me that he was cheating on me. This revelation rocked my entire world to the core. I was really devastated. I started crying so uncontrollably that I had to go into the bathroom stall so that I wouldn't ruin the birthday fun. I cried because there was nothing I could do. But shortly after, crying became rage. I was furious.

What had I done wrong? I did everything that Luis wanted me to do—even a few things that I really didn't want to do. I had lost my virginity to Luis, thinking it meant he loved me. So how could he turn around and do this to me?

It was a total betrayal. I could do nothing but just sit in the bathroom stall and cry until Isabel finally came to get me. As I ran some cool water on my face at the sink, she said that Drake would take us home. As we left the bathroom, I picked up a few extra napkins to both wipe away the remaining water and hide my face from my obvious emotional breakdown.

I managed to pull myself together enough to make it out the door. Thank goodness I did not see Luis as I was leaving. Otherwise, I would have made a fool of myself trying to fight him in Haunted Trails surrounded by my friends.

When we got into the car, Drake told me to sit in the front with him so that he could try to cheer me up. But I knew that nothing he could say was ever going to make me feel good that night. As I sat in the front seat, Drake leaned over immediately and tried to kiss me. He was a big eighteen-year-old and I was merely fourteen. One part of me wondered what this older boy would want with me and another part of me thought, *Wow, this eighteen-year-old likes me.*

As we drove along, Isabel asked if we could pull into the gas station so that she could pick up a pack of cigarettes—and Drake pulled right over. As I watched Isabel walk into the station, I was thinking about maybe going in myself to get something. Suddenly, I felt the heavy weight of Drake's body, leaning again in my direction. He started kissing me and I let him. There was a small part of me that felt that if I went along with it, I was secretly stabbing Luis in the back—true revenge. I started to kiss him back. I had absolutely no idea how this all would play out, but I knew it wasn't going to be good.

We stopped kissing as soon as Isabel got back into the car and we drove the rest of the way home in silence. When we got to Isabel's house, Drake told Isabel to go upstairs once he realized that her parents weren't at home. Isabel just abandoned me without question. My stomach turned over, watching her back disappear up the stairs.

Didn't she know how upset I was about Luis? Or how aggressive Drake was? She just walked away, leaving me standing there with Drake, who I didn't even know was staying. When I had gotten into the car with them, I thought it was just for a ride back to Isabel's house. The make out session at the gas station had already left me feeling guilty and ashamed. I wasn't interested in any more time with Drake.

Once Isabel went up the stairs, Drake grabbed my hand and led me into Isabel's brother's bedroom. My voice went hoarse, and I couldn't seem to utter the word *no*. He quickly shut the door and began unzipping my pants. My chest tightened and my throat seemed to collapse, preventing any words from escaping my lips. I couldn't seem to move. It was like my body just went stiff and I lost all ability to control my limbs. He pushed me onto the bed.

What's happening? What's happening? What's happening? Where's Isabel?

Drake's face crept toward the space between my thighs. My legs were cold in contrast to his hot breath washing over my skin. He began to perform oral sex on me. It felt nice physically but not so nice emotionally. What was I doing letting Drake go down on me on the same day that I broke up with my boyfriend?

As he continued, I felt so numb and detached, as if I was

outside of myself looking down at a stranger. I had no idea how this was happening to me. I honestly didn't want it. Yet I had put myself in this situation and had no idea how to get out of it. This left me feeling upset with *myself*. I felt I had let this happen, giving him mixed signals in the car at the gas station. This was my fault. So, again, I went with it.

After about a minute, Drake started kissing my belly, my hips, and my breasts until he got to my mouth, where he stopped kissing me. Instead, he grabbed the back of my head and pushed it slightly downward, directing me toward his erect penis. I opened my mouth and began to reciprocate what he had done for me just moments earlier. But I was not proud of myself.

I knew that if Luis ever found out about this, he would be livid. That was what I focused on in order to get through whatever this was. I felt Drake's hands grip the back of my head, pushing in a rhythmic motion to guide me in how he wanted this to go down.

Within minutes, Drake was on top of me, and we were having intercourse, rough sex with no love or tenderness between us. He was simply trying to have an orgasm, and I was just the vessel he was using to make it happen. I felt dirty and used and disloyal, even though Luis had cheated on me. My doing this didn't make me feel any better. Instead, I was quite ashamed.

Once Drake climaxed, he got up and told me to get dressed. I complied without saying a single word as I rushed into the bathroom, where I immediately started bawling. I was spiraling out of control, having allowed myself to be totally abused.

Drake had taken full advantage of my vulnerability in a cruel, selfish way. Like many teenage boys, he was not only immature but idiotic and mean. This was such a low point for me. I was even embarrassed to tell Isabel what had happened. I washed the salty tear stains from my face, gargled with a bit of Listerine, and then went into Isabel's bedroom, where I fell asleep to the sound of my own sobs.

It was years before I recognized this moment for what it was—sexual assault. Years before I understood how pivotal this moment was to my understanding of my own self-worth or to explaining why I let myself be mistreated by so many men after Luis and Drake. I carried internal shame and self-loathing about that moment for a long time and see now that it influenced all the rebellious behavior and poor choices that came after it. Instead of seeing this experience for what it was, I suppressed it. And while it was there, suppressed in my subconscious, it picked away at my self-trust, self-esteem, and self-understanding. My self-destructive behavior had only just begun. I had absolutely no self-worth.

*   *   *   *   *

The next morning, my eyes were so puffy from crying myself to sleep that I could hardly open them. But I arose to the smell of sizzling sausages, which awakened my hunger. I got dressed and headed downstairs to find a scene of total normalcy—Isabel's family gathered around the table eating breakfast.

There they were, chattering away happily. But as soon as they saw me, the talking stopped. I immediately felt as if the conversation must have been about me. I said good morning to everyone but didn't get a response from anyone. *That was weird.*

I thought maybe no one heard me. But as I took my place at the table, one of Isabel's brothers uttered the Spanish word *sucia*, which means "dirty."

At that humiliating moment, I felt my stomach flip in embarrassment. Isabel's entire family knew exactly what I had done the previous night with Drake. And clearly, they were all talking about it around the breakfast table before I had woken up.

I wanted to crawl into a hole and just curl up in a ball of shame. But to my credit, I didn't do that.

I was a vulnerable teenager looking for the meaning of love, wanting to *feel* love in any way that I could. Love had been a difficult thing to define. I had thought love was the way my parents were during their balloon days. But those days had floated away and there was nothing left resembling them.

But the night with Drake hadn't been about looking for love at all. I was devastated that my boyfriend had been unfaithful. Then, in my vulnerable state, I became the victim.

The pain of this situation made me want to be even

more rebellious, not less. I was nothing like my brother, who complied with authority and got good grades. He didn't party. Nor did he have sex until he was much older than me. He chose the fixed, controlled, stay-out-of-trouble path. Perhaps that was his way to cope.

I did what I wanted to do and what I needed to do to mask my hurt and pain. If it took drugs, alcohol, and sex to help me escape reality, so be it. Those three things provided me some glimpse of pleasure. Destructive as it might have been, I did not see any of this back then.

I sat at the table that morning and tried my best to act as normal as possible. I could not believe that Drake had told everyone what I had done. Or was it Isabel who had told her entire family that I had slept with Drake? I'll never know.

I felt totally betrayed. And as if things could not possibly get worse, they did when Luis showed up! I couldn't understand why he was even at Isabel's house so early in the morning.

But from the angry expression on his face, he clearly knew all about the evening as well. He quickly entered the room, said hello to everyone and then came straight toward me with a scary look of intensity in his eyes. He then grabbed me by my hand and asked me to come with him so that we could talk privately. My heart was pounding at the idea of what was about to happen.

As we headed up to Isabel's room, I turned to see what everyone else was doing. They were all just staring at us.

As we reached Isabel's door, Luis pushed it open and kind of tugged my hand to pull me inside. He slammed the door and immediately looked at me with tears in his eyes and screamed, "Why? Why did you do that?!"

I didn't know what to say. I wanted to scream at him and tell him that the only reason I slept with Drake was to get back at him for cheating on me. But instead, I said nothing.

Luis was now screaming that it was Drake who had grabbed my ass at the birthday party, that Drake had actually made a bet with Luis saying that he was going to sleep with me. Luis swore he told Drake that I would never sleep with him because I was not the kind of girl who would cheat on him. He assured Drake that he could never get me in bed. Hearing how these two idiots were bartering about me made me sick.

But there was nothing I could do but cry.

He looked at me with disgust, a contemptuous expression that I had never before seen in his eyes. Truthfully, I felt the same way about myself. I had let myself down for allowing this to happen, and now I was losing Luis because of it. There was really nothing left for me to do but cry.

Luis and I were done. He walked out of the room, crying while proclaiming self-righteously that he never wanted to see me again. He was so hurt. And I was so ashamed that I could barely look at him, engulfed in self-pity and guilt, blaming myself for everything—for Luis cheating on me, for sleeping with Drake.

"You were right about one thing," Luis said in parting.

"I never knew what I had until it was gone."

What a mess.

The sexual assault, breakup with Luis, and Isabel's abandonment was a pivotal moment in my life. Unfortunately, it signified the downfall of my friendship with Isabel. That alone was tragic. She had been my best friend.

After I slept with Drake, there was just no way to heal the awkwardness between us. I certainly no longer felt comfortable hanging out at her house with her family, who clearly judged me harshly. I felt like they looked at me like I was a slut, and I felt like I had been used. The very word her family had used to describe me, *dirty*, was how I felt, and I couldn't shake that feeling anytime I was with Isabel.

The fact that she and her family saw it as a romantic encounter instead of an assault was infuriating and confusing. It cast doubt in my own mind about what happened that night, convincing me I had chosen sex with Drake and everything I was feeling was just guilt because I had "cheated" on Luis. Feeling entirely powerless, the only thing that seemed to be *in* my control was whether to continue hanging out with Isabel. I decided I couldn't and moved on from the friendship.

CHAPTER FIVE

When It Rains, It Pours

1992
Orland Park, Illinois

WITH ISABEL OUT of the picture, I went looking for a "replacement," another friend who could fill in the space. My new partner in crime was Carol. The two of us became inseparable, thick as thieves, totally devoted. There wasn't anything we wouldn't do for one another. She was "the real deal" in terms of her loyalty toward me, so she quickly became my best friend. And I put all my trust in her. Even though we were just fourteen years old, her parents weren't as strict as Isabel's had been, which gave Carol and I more opportunity to do as we pleased. There was no tying bedsheets together to sneak out of Carol's house; we just went where we pleased, when we pleased.

Carol had a steady boyfriend, Aaron, who lived in Chicago, which gave us the perfect excuse to ditch school and get on a bus so Carol could visit him. Skipping school became a regular thing for me. I loved it. But once my dad realized what was happening, he started calling my brother every morning to check on me like a detective.

"Did she actually leave for school?" he'd ask James.

Once I caught on to my dad's MO, I began pulling a few tricks out of my sleeve as well.

Little did my dad know that I would hide underneath my bed in the mornings until my brother left for school. That way, James wouldn't know where I was. He assumed that I actually went to school. My brother, always so naive and straight-and-narrow about everything, never thought to check under the bed.

"She must have left before I did, because she's already gone," he would tell my dad.

After James left the house, I would then walk to Carol's house. And from there our delinquent journey began: we would take three buses plus a train to get from Orland Park to the corner of Forty-Seventh and Halsted.

As soon as we got off the bus, there was Aaron waiting for us with a few joints rolled up and ready to be lit. Some of the best conversations we ever had were when we were stoned on weed, walking from the bus to his place. Our inhibitions vanished and we did nothing but laugh and talk about anything and everything.

One of our favorite hangout spots was a rec center for teens called The Emmy. This was for kids who had no other place to go. Its sole purpose was to keep kids off the streets, out of gangs, and off drugs. From the outside of the building, it looked like a giant house, but on the inside it was as large as an apartment complex. It was the perfect spot for us, comfortably decorated with lots of chairs and couches, a pool table, a homemade bowling alley, and a video game area too—equipped with all the latest games that we could play for free.

What we liked best of all was that the staff never asked questions about why we were there (and not in school), and they never judged us either. The people who worked there would give us snacks, help us with our homework, and always ask if we had a place to sleep for the night. No alcohol or drugs were allowed.

It was a safety net for a lot of kids whose home lives were challenging, neglectful, or abusive. Aaron's house was just down the street, but his stepfather was an alcoholic and they constantly got into physical altercations. The Emmy was a place to escape all of that, not that it worked in Aaron's case. He still found access to cocaine, robbed places, and ended up in jail for theft.

Carol and I spent more and more time in the center. I wish I could have gotten a few more of our friends to hang out there, too, because it was a safe haven from a lot of bull-shit that went down on the streets—the violent fights, racist attacks, robberies, sexual assault, stabbings, and drug use. We were taking our lives in our hands to do what we were doing. Although I had an ill-tempered, overworked father, at least he cared. So many teenagers had absentee parents who were neglectful, who really *didn't* care about taking care of them. And trust me, we were vulnerable and *all* needed protection. At the rec center, we could congregate and feel safe.

As time passed, Aaron's friend Luke started coming to the rec center, too, which opened up more opportunities for the four of us to hang out together. Luke was seventeen, lean, and blond. He was from Canaryville, another rough neighborhood to grow up in. The camaraderie between the four of us felt great and created an opening for a new relationship between me and Luke. It started with Luke flirting with me a lot.

I think he flirted with *everyone*, but I didn't care. I was single and I loved every minute of the attention I was getting from him. I would flirt back. Sometimes, since Aaron's parents were almost never home, we started hanging out at his house too. It was cool for us to be there while everyone else was at school. The one thing we had at Aaron's house that we didn't have at the rec center was privacy.

It was party time, a respite from the sober rules of the rec center. We all just kind of lazed around his living room, getting drunk and smoking weed until we couldn't function properly. But we played it cool cause you would get kicked out if anyone knew.

One night while hanging out at Aaron's house, we totally lost track of time and wound up missing the last bus home. For sure, I knew my absence was going to be a big issue with my dad. So I called to let him know that I was okay and that he shouldn't worry at all because I was staying over at a friend's house. But my quick excuse didn't help the situation at all.

The conversation with Dad made me feel quite guilty because I could hear the sadness in his voice as I told him that I wasn't coming home that night. I loved my dad and didn't want to see him hurt by my actions. But he never showed interest in spending any time with me, nor did he have the energy to, so I didn't think he would miss me.

As it turned out, my dad had been really worried because he had no idea where I was, and he had already been informed by the school that I had missed all my classes that day. As a mother now, I see that any parent would be sick with worry. There were many times to come when I stayed out all night and never even called my dad, making him wonder whether I was dead or alive. It must have been truly horrible for him. But as a teenager, I was selfish and willful, oblivious to all boundaries.

The irony is that I *did* feel safe in Aaron's house, surrounded by friends who I felt would never hurt me. So as sad as my dad sounded on the phone, I decided that it was best for me to stay at Aaron's house that night. We had fun talking until we all passed out.

The next morning, as Carol and I were getting ready to leave Aaron's house, I realized there was a group of teenage girls waiting outside of Aaron's house ready to beat my ass.

What I didn't know was that Luke apparently had a girlfriend, who wasn't too pleased with me because of the attention I was getting from him. I know what I would have done to another girl who was trying to steal my boyfriend, so I could only imagine how angry this girl was.

Katherine had decided that *this* was the day that she and her friends were going to set the record straight and punish me for hooking up with her boyfriend. They were going to make sure that I stayed the hell away from Luke for good. This fight was unfair. It was me against a group of angry girls, so it wasn't going to turn out well.

For the first time in my life, I felt panicked and had no idea what to do. I had never actually gotten into a physical fight with another girl before, much less a group of them, and it wasn't something I wanted to do now.

At first, Carol and I decided we were going to hide inside Aaron's house until we figured out what to do. When I told a sleepy-looking Luke what was going on outside, he seemed unbothered by it. In fact, I believe I saw a smile stretch across his face. I think he was a little amused that girls were fighting over him. It appealed to his ego. But he also didn't want us to get jumped.

So Aaron turned to his mother for help. She was pissed at the situation happening outside her house and got up and gave Carol and me a ride to the train station so that we didn't have to walk outside past those girls. We left the house through the backyard and went directly to the garage so we didn't have to cross paths with Katherine and her gang.

As we drove past the group of girls outside, I couldn't help but flash a smile in Katherine's direction. I knew it was wrong, but I did it anyway. I wanted her to know that I was laughing inside at how stupid she looked on the outside. I wanted her to know that even though Luke was her man, she wasn't going to "get" me that day.

And even though I had never slept with Luke, I wanted her to hate me and know that if I *wanted* to sleep with him, I could have. I don't know why I had such animosity in my heart toward this girl I didn't even know. Instead, I should have been pissed at Luke for double-dating.

My moment of triumph was short-lived.

When I got back home, I felt shitty about how I had treated my father, regretting how sad he was as a result of my actions. I decided that I needed to go back to school and start applying myself again. It was my freshman year; he and Mom were already talking about my life after high school. The least I could do was show him that I was trying and that I wasn't a total screwup. But even though I refocused and made a resolution to try harder, my return to school entailed a lot of unwanted drama.

On the day I returned to school, the dean of academic affairs was waiting for me. After sitting down in a seat for my first class of the day, I heard the dean calling my teacher over the intercom and requesting that I come down to his office at once. I was confused. How could I possibly be in trouble for something when I just got to class? Of course, it was beyond my realm of thinking to link my delinquent attendance record to now being called on the carpet.

I grabbed my backpack and headed down to the office, where the dean was waiting with his door open for me. He asked me to have a seat and he quickly relayed the message that my father was on his way to the school and that the police were also coming to speak with me. *The police?! What? Why?* At this point, the theme song for my life matched the saying "When it rains, it pours."

With a straight face, a police officer began to explain to me that I was in deep trouble due to my attendance record—and that I was headed to prison if I didn't straighten up. Talk about overkill. He then handed me a sheet of paper, an agreement that he wanted me to sign—a condition for me not getting arrested. It stated that if I didn't stop ditching school to hang out with my friends, and that if I didn't cut off my friendship with Carol (a bad influence), I would be sent to a juvenile detention center, a mental facility, where I would receive mandatory treatment. I could not believe this!

The dean added that I "needed help" and that my behavior had led to this moment. I knew, of course, that I had been a problem child, ditching school and staying out late to party. But I was not mentally ill! In that facility, yes, there might have been kids who suffered from mental illness, but I was just rebellious. I was 100 percent sane and couldn't believe that the threat of sending me to a mental institution was a part of this agreement that the school dean was forcing on me.

I started suspiciously thinking that this situation reeked of my mother's input, that she had called the dean and convinced him to act and put together this ridiculous agreement. I didn't believe that my father would ever do this. Maybe he called Mom and told her about all my partying, and this was the result. Otherwise, there was no way the dean would come up with this threatening punishment all on his own.

I was infuriated. I thought, *How can my mother sandbag me like this when she was the one that left me to fend for myself?* Over the years, she'd been back and forth from Chicago to Tennessee, with and without Justin, time and time again. Her life had been chaos, to say the least. And now she was judging me! This was the ultimate betrayal, a punitive measure taken by the very person who abandoned me.

I was taken with my dad to the police station, my mom met us there, and hours passed. While we were there, my mom told me it was my dad who reached out to the police and asked for help because he was literally scared for my life. And yes, he had called up my mom and told her all about it. She had agreed with him, but she pointed the finger at him as being solely responsible. He was furious with her for not backing his decision and throwing him under the bus. Having believed it was my mother who had called the police, not my dad, learning the truth put me over the edge. I went straight into a rage because Dad lied to me, and I refused to sign the agreement. I now understand that he was just trying to help me, but I couldn't wrap my head around that at the time. He told me that I should just sign the paper so we could go home. I finally did sign it, agreeing that I would not see Carol anymore. But I agreed to it only so I could get the hell out of that police station.

As soon as we left, I was determined to defy the agreement. After all, it was a Friday night and I had already planned to spend it at Carol's house with Aaron and Luke. So the second my dad started driving me home, I reminded him that I was going ahead with seeing Carol. He couldn't believe it and tried to convince me not to do it, knowing that I was going to get into even more trouble. To manipulate him, I reminded him that I didn't do anything wrong.

I was not taking no for an answer. That night, I went with Carol to meet Luke and Aaron at the bus station. We walked around the mall and to the park, where we all smoked, and then went and snuck our dates into Carol's bedroom. I guess we were a little loud, so her dad came down and started screaming, telling our boyfriends to get out.

He called the cops for good measure to ensure they left and probably to try to ensure these older guys had nothing more to do with his daughter. But if they were leaving, so were we. We left when they did.

The cops found us walking around past curfew and took us into the police station. We weren't doing anything wrong by just walking the street, but the cops were making good on the call they received from Carol's dad. They brought us all in and started calling our parents one by one.

Now I was really screwed. I was so angry and felt I had not done anything wrong. I mean, what's the big deal? It was a teenage sleepover.

Aaron and Luke were released and had to make their way back to Chicago. Carol's dad picked her up. My dad arrived, and then things took a drastic turn.

The police called Hartgrove, a hospital for troubled teens, just as they had threatened to do. It had been written inside that blasted agreement. An attendant soon arrived, strapping me to a stretcher like I was insane. Dad jumped in the ambulance with me and promised that he wouldn't leave me. Mom was on her way and would meet us there.

When we all arrived at the hospital, they released me from the stretcher. A Hartgrove staff member took us for a tour of the building. Then it was decision time. Would my parents make good on their threat and commit me? Did they really think they could scare me straight?

I was totally opposed to staying in that facility. Leaving me there was just not happening. So my dad forced them to release me. "But next time you pull some shit," he warned, "this is where you're going to end up!"

Where was all this leading?

CHAPTER SIX

Irresistible Drama

1993–1994
Orland Park, Illinois

AFTER THE TOUR of the institution, I stayed out of trouble very briefly, attempting to avoid the people I had been hanging out with prior to being threatened with Hartgrove. I went to school and then came home, keeping my head down. But my desire to stay sober was shaky.

It took only a few days of following the dull routine at school to realize I was not going to be able to keep up with *that* schedule. By the middle of the week, I broke down and called Carol to see what she was up to. Of course, she immediately told me to skip school and drop by the mall because that's where she wanted to hang out. I hadn't been there in what seemed like forever, so I took a shower, got dressed, and headed out.

When I got to the mall, Carol was with Rachel, a casual acquaintance. Rachel was in a teenage drama fit, angry that her boyfriend had slept with a girl who was also at the mall that day. We knew that a cat fight or a brawl was about to happen. Rachel walked toward the girl, screaming all the profanities she could think of, while I charged behind her to lend support. Even though I knew doing this violated my promise to stay out of trouble, I did it anyway, knowing it was possible I could wind up at Hartgrove for much longer than a tour of the grounds.

Then, before the girl in question even got a chance to respond, Rachel grabbed a handful of the girl's hair, balled up her fist, and punched that girl in the face. The next thing I knew, both of them were on the ground wrestling, while I was kicking and stomping on the girl. All this seems overblown and ridiculous as I think about it now, not to mention it being assault, but when you're a teenager, you don't stop and think about any of that when your friend is getting her ass kicked. Something about the drama is irresistible.

Almost as quickly as it started, it was over. Someone yelled, "Cops!" and everyone ran in different directions. Eventually, my friends and I met back up and gravitated toward a circle of teenagers in the distance, and we found ourselves standing on the outskirts looking in.

In the center of the circle was a super fit Puerto Rican guy named Logan, whom we had seen at the roller rink not that long ago. He was a bodybuilder type with huge muscles, a six-pack—the works. Turns out he was an incredible dancer. He was showing off his moves and doing cartwheels. Clearly everyone thought he was fly, including himself.

When Logan took a break from dancing, he went over to chat with another cute boy, Kirk, who happened to be his cousin. We recognized him from the roller rink too. As Logan went back to dance, both Rachel and I kept our eyes locked on Kirk, hoping he might notice us.

When the dancing was done and the group started to disband, some of us headed into the arcade and played games for a while. Logan and Kirk competed in the way guys do to get girls to notice them—roughhousing, talking over one another, subtly glancing in our direction to see if we were paying attention. We attempted to look uninterested.

Eventually, Rachel, Carol, and I got ready to leave the mall. Rachel went her way, waving goodbye. Then, as Carol and I were about to jump into a car with some random guys for a ride home, Logan came up to me and asked if his cousin Kirk could have my number. He suggested that I take a ride with them instead.

We left with the cousins and went cruising for a while. They got us some malt liquor and then asked if they could sleep over at Carol's house. Carol said yes, and we ended up sneaking them in through the window. I'll never forget Kirk and I making out that night; Carol and Logan hooked up as well.

After falling asleep, Kirk and I were both awakened at 4:00 a.m. to the sound of Carol crying. Aaron was currently in jail, and she felt incredibly guilty for having hooked up with Kirk even though it was impossible for her to spend any time with Aaron while he was incarcerated. While I felt for Carol, I was still reeling from my epic make out with Kirk just a few hours before.

Before Kirk and Logan left late that morning, Kirk gave me a kiss goodbye and asked what time I would be off work at The Potato Factory later that day. The Potato Factory was one of the dining options at the food court in the mall, and I had been working there for only about six months. It's a wonder I kept that job as long as I did given how uncommitted I was to attending school. Kirk promised he would pick me up after my shift and we would do something special.

Though I barely knew him, there was a lot to love about him from my adolescent perspective. He was super fine. He had a car, a job, and money to spend. While he was much older—seventeen and working as a welder, while I was just fourteen—it never occurred to me that our age difference might be a problem. Kirk's interest in me was immediate, and that was all I needed. Deep down I still felt haunted by what happened with Drake. The shame from that event was still crushing my self-esteem. Falling into infatuation with Kirk was an easy way to feel wanted and to forget how dirty I felt about Drake.

As promised, when my shift ended that evening, Kirk was right there. He slipped his arm around my shoulders and leaned in.

"Come here. Let me buy you something nice." His words

landed softly in my ear and sent tingles down my spine. We walked to the nearest jewelry store that we all referred to as the gold shop. It wasn't as nice as a Kay's or Jared's, but at that point, no one had ever bought me a piece of jewelry. The fact I was taken into *any* jewelry store was a big deal.

"Go ahead. Pick something out," he said as he leaned against one of the glass cases.

"Really? Anything?" I asked, trying not to grin from ear to ear.

He nodded and watched me.

I weaved in and out of the cases scanning the rings for something that I liked until I came across a gold band with an engraved rose.

"That one," I said, pointing.

He waved one of the store clerks over to retrieve the ring, slapped down cash, and slid the ring onto my finger. I was in love!

I spent that night at his dad's house (though his dad was nowhere to be seen). As always, my parents were calling everyone they knew to find me, but I was in a world of my own. I spent the next day chilling at Kirk's house while he was at work.

At lunchtime, a girl knocked on the back door, identifying herself as Kirk's sister, Wendy. Weirdly, she came in, took a whole bunch of his clothes, and then left.

"Tell Kirk that Wendy stopped by," she said, closing the door behind her and glaring at me as she walked away.

When Kirk got home, he asked what happened to his clothes.

"Your sister took them," I told him.

He exploded. "I don't have a sister!" Completely enraged, he grabbed a bat and said, "Let's go."

I followed him to his car and jumped into the passenger side. I probably should have been concerned about the bat and the eruptive outburst, but as far as I was concerned some chick had stolen his stuff and she deserved whatever was coming.

He pulled up at a house and popped the trunk on her car. All his clothes were inside. Kirk grabbed them and tossed them into his car. Then he busted out the windows of the vehicle. He jumped back in the car and peeled away. He was pissed. Clearly, this was a girl he was in a relationship with.

"I have to take you home," he said.

"Let me call Carol first," I told him, and we drove until we found a pay phone.

At this point, I had been gone nearly forty-eight hours. My parents hadn't seen me since I headed to the mall for my shift at The Potato Factory, and they hadn't a clue where I was. They had called every friend they knew to call, and I wasn't with any of them. They didn't yet know about Kirk.

Due to my unknown whereabouts, I had been officially reported as a runaway and the cops were looking for me. When I called Carol to ask about going to her place, she told me I couldn't head that way because the cops were already looking for me at her house. There was nothing to do but have Kirk drop me off down the street from my house so I could face the consequences.

When I stepped inside, my parents were both there. They immediately took me to the car and drove me directly to Hartgrove. Inside the car, I pulled the seat belt tightly around me. With the belt securely fastened, I felt some ounce of protection. Like somehow the belt would magically lock me in the car and protect me from being taken back to the hospital. It didn't work; there was no magic to keep me trapped in the car and safe from Hartgrove.

But eventually I had to get out the car and face reality. I knew that this time around, I would be admitted. I remember thinking that I had just found the "perfect" guy and then *this*. I was incredibly upset and couldn't stop crying. In between the sobs, I heard my parents speaking with the front desk and one of the staff members. Papers were signed.

As I was led away, I could hardly see where I was going because my vision was so blurred by my tears. My parents left. I was officially admitted, as I knew I would be.

That first night I was so distraught that the staff had me on suicide watch, which meant I had to sleep in the hallway so they could observe me. As I lay there, I felt abandoned and trapped, but I knew I had to calm down and control myself. Otherwise, I would wind up strapped down in one of the padded rooms for patients who could not control their behavior.

*   *   *   *   *

During that first week, it was one group session after another, meeting people who had serious mental health disorders. Some were suicidal, others just rebellious or depressed, and then there were those who were straight-up crazy. One girl confided that she was a devil worshiper and made animal sacrifices, telling us about some horrible things she did to those poor creatures. I thought to myself, *I don't need to be here! I'm not crazy!* I rebelled and refused to participate in those group-therapy sessions. I just didn't care about *anything*. I was going to do what I wanted to do, period. I was so angry.

My first weekend at Hartgrove, my dad came to visit. We were brought to a table in the corner of a larger room. Other kids were visiting with family as we took our seats across from each other. I was so furious with him for doing this to me, I didn't want to talk to him. I was incapable of recognizing how my actions were what led to this outcome.

"How you doin'?" he asked.

I began to cry. "I don't need to be locked up in here," I said through sniffles.

Just then, Logan walked in, and my mood completely shifted.

My dad glared at this giant young man. I think he expected Logan to walk by us and prove he was there to visit someone else. When he stopped at our table, my dad looked from him to me and back to him again.

"And you are?" Dad asked, standing up, his feathers ruffled.

"Logan. I came to see Jen," he said, hardly looking at him. Logan turned to me and softened. "Kirk sends a message." (Kirk was sitting in the car outside and wasn't allowed in to visit since he wasn't an adult, so he sent Logan in to deliver his sentiments.)

My dad crossed his arms.

"He wanted me to tell you he loves you," Logan said.

Out of the corner of my eye I saw my dad rub his face with one hand. I tried not to smile, knowing my dad was growing impatient with this whole thing. He must have been wondering who the hell Kirk was too.

"How about a hug before I go?" Logan asked.

I leaned into his huge arms and chest. For a moment, I wished he could conceal me enough to sneak me out—more magical thinking that was useless.

As Logan was heading out the door, I saw Kirk standing on the other side. He had begged security to let him in so that he could give me a hug. I ran to the door. We hugged and I held on tightly, feeling safe in his arms for those brief moments. Then they left. I returned to the table with Dad and sat back down. I turned on the waterworks again. I needed to get out of there and back to Kirk. I began begging for my release, swearing I would behave, knowing full well I wouldn't. I was such a manipulator.

Dad explained that my treatment team was not inclined to let me out yet. My release would depend on my commitment to intensive outpatient therapy. After several minutes of arguing, I agreed to the program. I just wanted to get out of that place and away from those crazy people. I was out of control, but I wasn't crazy.

On the tenth day, I was allowed to leave—when the insurance company wouldn't continue paying for my treatment. Still, the terms of my release were that I had to commit to attending a thirty-day intensive outpatient behavioral program at Christ Hospital designed for kids like me who had "anger issues." This didn't sound much better than Hartgrove, but at least we were allowed to go home each evening.

Once the program began, we settled into the routine and did our schoolwork under supervision while also attending group therapy multiple times a day. On our break, we got to go down to the cafeteria to eat, and a few of us would head to the parking garage to smoke cigarettes. Newport menthol cigarettes were so good, and they helped to relieve my stress. Looking back, I realize that relying on cigarettes as a coping strategy before I was even old enough to buy them was not a healthy choice.

The thing that still stands out the most about my time at Christ Hospital was the punching bag on the wall—the perfect therapy for kids like us who were presumably boiling in anger. I couldn't really pinpoint anger as my issue, but I loved punching that bag. What a release! But the group sessions felt like a waste of time, and I refused to find any use in them. There was no form of therapy that would have worked at that point, because I wasn't invested in my own growth.

I wasn't ready for a change, and no one seemed to be interested in getting to the root of my behavioral issues. Everyone wanted to talk about what I was doing and why it was wrong. No one really dug deep to address *why* I was doing any of these things in the first place. Because my dad appeared to genuinely care about me (by his persistence in finding me help like Hartgrove and Christ Hospital), no one would have guessed what he was like at home. No one knew he was part of the problem.

His explosive temper, his put-downs, and his swearing at me for small infractions regularly destroyed my self-esteem and sense of self-worth. He always made me feel not good enough and not worthy of his love. And it was clear that he valued his material possessions more than his relationships with his kids or others. But I didn't know any of this then. I just knew that when I was with people like Carol, I felt loved and accepted and like I belonged somewhere. So it didn't matter what I was doing. I just wanted to be with people who wanted to be with me.

During my thirty-day program, Kirk and Logan would come to visit me at home after I returned for the day. Logan had a girlfriend named Katherine, and they had a baby named Maria, so they would sometimes bring her along. My dad didn't like when they all came over. He thought they were bad influences, and I had just turned fifteen, while Kirk was going on eighteen.

We would spread out in the living room and hang out, and sometimes we'd make cinnamon rolls in the kitchen, which gave me that warm, family-like feeling I craved. The smell of the rolls rising in the oven made me think of those weekends when my brother and I had time with our dad. The weekends that were carefree and uncomplicated. The days when it felt like the three of us were against the world but that if we had each other, it would be okay. We felt more like a family then.

*   *   *   *   *

To my credit, I finished my outpatient therapy program. I cooperated because I was afraid that if I didn't, they would lock me back up. I went each day and followed the rules while I was there. I listened to what they had to say, but I didn't speak during therapy sessions. Although I was on my best behavior while under their magnifying glass, I was always thinking about what I would get up to when it was all over.

Despite that, completing the requirements did offer a small amount of positive reinforcement for my self-esteem (though I never felt like I should have been in there in the first place). It proved that I could follow through and commit to things, which would come into play later in life. I just didn't know it yet.

Once I was through the program and released "back

into the wild," I resumed my usual activities. It was more like a sixty-day time-out had finally ended. Nothing had really changed.

Kirk was consistently hanging around the house. His presence irritated my dad, who informed me that Kirk had to stay away. This led to breaking up with Kirk but then making up and getting together again. This breaking up and getting back together was a never-ending loop, the way a lot of unhealthy adolescent relationships tend to be.

During one of our brief breakup periods, Kirk started hanging out with his ex-girlfriend again, and that infuriated me. So I often took off to Kirk's house for hours at a time to keep an eye on him.

My obsession with dating Kirk and wanting to be where the fun (and trouble) was made it impossible to focus on school. No matter how hard I tried, I just went back to my old ways. I know now it's because I felt like that's where I belonged. I gravitated toward those rebellious friends who were anything but good for me, all because they at least liked me.

*   *   *   *   *

With the outpatient program over, my parents were adamant that I return to school. I had absolutely no choice in the matter even though I would have preferred to quit school and get a job. It was either finish high school or my parents would find a way to put me back in Hartgrove. There was no way that was ever going to happen again.

In some ways I was looking forward to returning to normal school, if for no other reason than seeing all my old friends. Anything was better than Hartgrove or Christ Hospital. Going back would be refreshing in comparison to the fluorescent white walls, locked corridors, and crazed whisperings I had experienced in my two stints before.

My parents got the ball rolling and attempted to have me reregistered at my old high school, but that task was not as simple as it seemed. Between cutting classes, being locked up in a mental institution, and attending a thirty-day outpatient program, I had missed a lot of schoolwork. I had straight Fs in every class my sophomore year and was told that it would be impossible for me to catch up and move on to my junior year with the rest of my class. The principal told me and my parents that if I were to come back to school at all, I would have to *repeat* my entire sophomore year. In addition, he informed us that I would be listed as a "high risk" student. This meant that if I did anything wrong, if I so much as sneezed without permission, I would be expelled immediately with no questions asked.

My worst nightmare was repeating a grade. I could not imagine the shame and embarrassment I'd feel being left behind by all my friends. I would look like an idiot, stuck in classes with kids who were a year younger. Everybody would know. I'd be an outcast, treated like a loser.

My parents had no choice but to send me to an

alternative school called Benjamin Braun, a high school that was specifically created for the "troubled teens" in the area with mental, behavioral, and emotional disorders. Benjamin Braun would allow me to begin where I had left off regardless of how many classes I had missed during my sophomore year. I could still graduate the year I was supposed to. This school was my only option.

My parents were hopeful about sending me to a prison-style school, as they believed I would get the kind of treatment I needed. They believed I was not yet ready to return to a regular high school. Perhaps they felt guilty that my treatment at Hartgrove had been cut short. In their minds, this was the perfect solution. For me, this was an opportunity to prove they were wrong and that I didn't belong in some alternative program.

On the first day, as we pulled up in front of the school, my determination nearly disappeared as I gazed at the exterior. It was an old redbrick building. Boxy. Unwelcoming. And with the security guards carrying weapons at the front doors, it looked more like a prison than a school. I stepped out of the car and looked over my shoulder. Were they thinking the same thing I was about this place? Were they at all nervous that maybe this wasn't the right place for me?

Students walking into the building had to get by the security guards and the large metal detector positioned at the entrance. For a split second, I thought about turning around and walking away. My parents had already split, so there was no one to see me head the opposite direction. But before I got the chance to even consider which direction to escape, a guard approached me and instantly escorted me inside. They were not playing around.

As I discovered, most of the kids in class were on Ritalin, a medication used to treat attention deficit hyperactivity disorder. During a typical school day, nurses would come around to each classroom with medication, drugging students to keep them calm. Other kids (unmedicated) were completely out of control and probably would've behaved better on meds, but they would just hide the pills under their tongues.

On many occasions, out-of-control kids would lose it and literally flip their desks over, screaming at teachers and staff. Then guards rushed into the room, subduing that student with a variety of body holds. I may have done some things in my teenage life that were unsuitable, but these kids had me beat.

Punishment for bad behavior wasn't the same as at a normal high school. Instead of detention, we would be sent to a "time-out" pod, a small room with absolutely nothing in it. Just four bare walls. I figured it was their version of solitary confinement. If you weren't sent there, you were sent to an "adjustment" room, which had padding on the walls so you could be as crazy as you'd like and at least have something soft to run into. Between the two types of punishment rooms, the metal detectors, the guards, and the ways kids were subdued,

Benjamin Braun was as close to a prison as I ever wanted to be. I swore to myself that I would never end up in a real one.

I came to learn that many of the students came from abusive households, which influenced their foul tempers and tendency toward violence. I felt for these other kids, and it made me consider my own past experiences and traumas differently. My life, including my own choices and those of others, wasn't perfect. People made mistakes and hurt me, and I hurt others also. However, I feel lucky that I wasn't ever beaten. My parents loved me in their messed-up ways and had tried to help me as best they knew how, even if putting me in Hartgrove (and then Christ Hospital and then Benjamin Braun) had felt really messed up. (The truth is, as a parent now, I have no idea what I would have done with a child like me. I know they were doing all they could, but unfortunately it wasn't enough.)

Watching the chaos at Benjamin Braun swirl around me made me wonder, *Why am I hurting? What's my story?* Although I was in an environment for troubled and ill-behaved teens, I didn't believe I was a bad person. I just felt misunderstood or misguided. Maybe both. Again, no one was really helping me sort through my feelings or get to the root cause of them.

I believed everyone I met there was just broken in one way or another. But instead of the medical staff patiently working through our trauma and helping us heal, it was easier for them to put us all on meds and label us with psychiatric disorders. In reality, the parents were the root of these kids' trauma, but no one was working on the parents. Each time I got out of one of these facilities, things got worse. I felt ready to explode.

I had been using alcohol and drugs and sex to cope with how I felt, but I wasn't suffering from a serious mental illness. In fact, my biggest issue at the time was my frustration. I didn't understand why I was hurting so much, or at least I couldn't put it into words. As a fifteen-year-old, I couldn't understand what was happening around me or to me. Something wasn't right, but as it all was happening, I couldn't explain it. Even now, I can't understand how all these doctors with all their degrees and intense therapies never got to the real issues and helped me find the words for what I was feeling. With all my time spent in therapeutic facilities during the worst years of my adolescence, you would think they would have. The fact is, so many of the people in these healing roles have their own trauma to understand and recover from. But if they don't do their own healing work, how can they really be in service to others?

The cost of being locked up in that facility was around $1,000 per day, some of which was being paid for by insurance. Honestly, I'm not sure how my parents afforded it for as long as they did. For such a high cost in both my time and in my parents' money, you would think healing would be a guarantee listed in the brochure. I honestly can't say any of us who attended were healed. It was more like biding our time.

The silver lining was that my best friend, Carol, attended

the same school, so at least I was not there alone. Isabel's ex-boyfriend also attended the school, and eventually the three of us formed a clique. We made our way through the school as a trio that could not be separated. We believed in each other, and that sense of camaraderie really helped us. Otherwise, I think being in that school would have driven me insane. More than anything, what I needed was someone to *believe* in me. And it was my small group of friends that got me through it.

We were all just broken and self-destructing young people, using sex, alcohol, drugs, violent behavior, and anything else we could in order to hide the pain we all had buried inside. We were all young people who hadn't been taught how to process difficult experiences in healthy ways. The only way to cope was to act out. The only way to be seen and heard was to self-destruct and seek negative attention. The only way to feel love and belonging was to find it in each other, even if we were a jumble of poor influences. We were the blind leading the blind. If there was one thing all of us at Benjamin Braun were really lacking, it was that sense of love from the people we wanted it from the most. We wanted to know we meant something to someone at home and that we were worthy of that love. At least this was true for me. What I wanted was loving attention from my family and a willing-ness to have the hard conversations so that we could get past our problems rather than keep them all bottled up.

My parents couldn't see how their own behaviors had

contributed to my misbehavior or how their focus on their own worlds meant they weren't paying attention to mine. My mom choosing her boyfriend over us had always felt like complete abandonment and selfishness. The way my dad spoke to us in the few moments we saw him each day when he wasn't working felt borderline abusive and was even more damaging than I could comprehend at that time.

I was a kid. I couldn't really express the way my parents' decisions had made me feel or how they influenced my behavior. To me, I was out of control in the same ways the my peers were, which made it seem acceptable. All teenagers rebel against their parents, right? This was the way I justified my behavior.

I didn't see any of it as a desperate cry for help or attention. I thought I was just doing normal teenager stuff and there was nothing motivating me to change. My parents paid attention only when I was getting into trouble, and they never seemed to think I was capable of anything else. So what did it matter if I applied myself to these programs or chose to abide by all the rules? They wouldn't care more just because I was going to school or getting good grades or hanging out with better kids.

No one could stop me but me. Only I could care enough about the direction I was headed to make different choices. And that would take some time and a huge wake-up call. Going to Benjamin Braun wasn't it.

I didn't have any other choice yet; I was genuinely trying

to change my life for the better. I was determined to graduate high school and make a better life for myself. And in my mind, getting my father's approval was key. I never felt good enough for him. So for my father's sake I would tough it out and try to make the best of this situation at such a tough school.

I did everything necessary to get an early release. I applied myself and my grades were much improved. And I began going home every day after school to further prove to my father that I really was trying to change for the better. I even picked up an extra class at the local college so that I could graduate with my class.

Unfortunately, other forces were pulling me back down. Friends were constantly trying to get me to hang out with them after school just to "unwind" from the stress of the day. I had to be careful about that because I couldn't fall into a pattern of skipping class, drinking, smoking pot, or staying up all night anymore. It was difficult to say no to them, but I was on a mission. I wanted my father to begin to trust me again.

There was just one major problem: my teenage romantic relationships began to pull me in the wrong direction. Again.

As I began attending the alternative school program, my relationship with Kirk took a turn for the worse. It seemed like all we ever did was fight and argue over small issues. At times, I didn't even know what we were fighting about. I think most of the arguing came from the fact that I couldn't spend as much time with him as I used to because of this new school structure.

There was no more being laid-back about school. Both my parents and the school were strict about my attendance. I had to attend Monday through Friday. Detentions were served during the day for those of us who veered off course. I decided it might be easier if I just did what I was told as far as school was concerned.

My regular attendance, paired with getting a part-time job (so I could have a little money to do the things I wanted), meant that my free time for hanging out with Kirk was far less than it had been. This wasn't ideal for Kirk, and though I missed him, I was tired of being punished by adults in my life. I was determined to stay the course for the rest of the school year at the very least.

*   *   *   *   *

Finally, summer came, and I could spend as much time as I wanted with Kirk. This didn't prove to be a good thing.

At one point during July, I disappeared from home for more than a week. I had been holed up at Kirk's house. My parents must have suspected where I was after a period of time, because one afternoon Kirk and I were driving down 147th Street when a car sped up next to us. I looked over and saw my dad. I was mortified.

Kirk pulled over and my father dragged me out of the

car as if he were saving me from a kidnapper. After Dad forced me into his car, he walked around to Kirk's side of the car.

Kirk's window was rolled down. Dad reached in through the window and grabbed Kirk by the collar of his shirt.

"Just you wait. One of these days I'm going to beat your ass." He shoved Kirk into his seat.

This was my dad's breaking point. He decided he was going to make sure Kirk and I were separated once and for all. And he did everything in his power to keep his word.

He refused to drive me anywhere, assuming I would end up at Kirk's house somehow. If I brazenly asked to go there, promising to be good and come home, he refused. If Kirk called the house, Dad told him I couldn't speak to him or that I was tied up or not there. Dad wouldn't even relay messages Kirk left for me. Intensifying the situation was the fact that Kirk had turned eighteen, and my dad recognized that if Kirk tried to have sex with me, it would now be statutory rape. I never really knew if my dad suspected (or knew) we already had sex or why it now mattered if it hadn't been a concern before.

Despite my father's efforts, I stayed connected to Kirk. If my dad wasn't around, I would call Kirk up or find out what was happening with him through my friends or his. And it was through Kirk's friends that I heard he was back with his ex-girlfriend and lying to me about it. In a rage, I cut off all communication and refused to speak with him.

A few weeks into my silent treatment, relay messages

Kirk left for me started making up all kinds of stories to capture my attention. For example, he told me he had been in a car accident and they shaved his head, saying he had to have brain surgery. He had an unbelievable reason as to why there was no scar. The day after that tall tale, he showed up at my house on crutches. Then, a couple of days later, I saw him walking around the mall with friends and there were no crutches in sight. Every time I challenged him on one of his half-baked stories, the only thing I ever accomplished was getting into another fight. I was convinced he was a compulsive liar, and those types only become enraged when you confront them on their lies.

We were on this merry-go-round together for several weeks.

Then one summer day, sometime in August, Kirk begged me to go back home with him because he claimed he had something for me. I knew he was lying about a gift, and I knew going to his place was explicitly forbidden by my father, but I went anyway. A part of me just wanted to believe he loved me and all this arguing and making up stories was just our way. So I ignored my gut feelings and let him drive me to his place.

When we got back to his house, we waved to his grandfather in the living room before we went to Kirk's bedroom. Kirk started to play video games and practically ignored me. It was his idea to come back to his place, and now it was like I wasn't even there.

I wanted to have sex, so I kept hinting at it. He just

continued to ignore me and play video games. When that didn't work, I started prodding him to tell me about this supposed gift.

"So where are you hiding it?" I asked, trying to be playful.

"The closet," he responded sharply, never taking his eyes off the TV.

I took a couple of steps toward the closet and began to open the door.

Kirk completely lost it.

He jumped off the bed, throwing the game controller, and slammed the closet door closed before I had it fully open. When I turned to look at him and poke fun at his overreaction, he put his hands around my neck and started choking me.

Kirk had never been violent toward me before. I had seen him blow out those car windows with a bat. I had seen him lose his temper on other people. I suspected that when I wasn't around, he got up to no good, and that included roughing some people up. But he had never laid a hand on me out of anger.

He kept me pinned against the closet door with his hand around my neck. I was terrified. He had this vacant expression, as if he wasn't even there. His eyes were blank and looking past me. I had never seen him look like that.

Then, he gripped my arms, turned me around, and pushed me onto the bed.

He pulled his pants down, hiked up my summer dress,

pushed my underwear out of the way, and forced himself inside of me. His thrusts were rough and sharp. That angry, dark, and vacant expression remained. I was truly afraid and cried. I couldn't seem to get out of his grasp, so I laid still, waiting for it to end, and felt the most horrific déjà vu. Again, I felt like I had floated out of my body and was looking down from the ceiling. Up there with me were ghosts from the night with Drake—shame, fear, guilt. I wondered if I had done something to deserve this.

Before Kirk climaxed, I could hear his grandfather from another room yelling at him to take me home. I was crying so loud, no wonder he could hear me. Maybe that was the old man's way of trying to stop what he assumed was happening. I'll never really know. His grandfather certainly didn't come into the room to intervene.

Kirk finally finished, and that absent look in his eyes disappeared. He seemed to return to himself. He began apologizing profusely, begging me to stay with him, but the damage was done. I was violated, and all I wanted to do was get away from him, but he laid on top of me to keep me from leaving.

I stood up, adjusted my dress, and wiped the tears from my face with the back of my hand.

"Take me home" were the only three words I could utter through my clenched jaw. "Now," I added as I headed for the door.

He blocked the door to his bedroom, desperate to resolve

things. "Please, Jen. I'm so sorry . . . Don't go . . ."

"If you don't take me home right now, my dad is going to call the police. I've got a curfew to keep."

I had never cared about my curfew before, and Kirk knew that. Kirk also knew it was quite possible my dad *would* call the police, especially if he found out I had been with Kirk. Given what just happened, I was certain Kirk was scared about the possibility and wondering what I might say if my dad asked.

Looking back on that moment, I recognize this was the second time I was raped. The fact that Kirk's grandfather heard my cries but did nothing to intervene has lingered with me all these years later.

As my own daughters have grown, I've remained vigilant and alert when boyfriends come over. I have listened for any aggressive remarks or violent tempers. I've taken note of any outrageous stories that don't make sense and have pointed out any discrepancies. I've taught my daughters that even partners can assault you, no matter how many times they tell you they love you or they're sorry. I also knew that the more you push them away from someone, the more they go towards them.

Once Kirk dropped me off at my dad's house, I waited for him to pull away. Then, I immediately went over to my mom's. I didn't want Kirk to know where I was. Because of his prior behavior, I knew it was unlikely he would just leave me alone. Plus, he had begged me the whole car ride to forgive him. My silence had unnerved him. When I got to my mom's house, I went immediately to my room and cried. I told no one what had happened.

Kirk must have followed me or found out through friends where I was, because the next day, he called my mom's house from the pay phone down the block. He told me he was coming to pick me up. We didn't have plans. I hadn't invited him over or asked to go out. He felt I was somehow his and he could order me around. I had no interest or intention of leaving with him or being alone with him.

I called my cousin to come pick me up. She came immediately and brought me back to her place. Ten minutes later, Kirk started calling her house instead. She told him I wasn't there. I've never figured out how he knew where I was or how he had her number. I just remember feeling scared by his persistence. He was stalking me, and I couldn't shake him.

Thankfully, my uncle knew something was wrong, so he answered the phone and told Kirk that I wasn't there. This still didn't stop him. Another ten minutes later, Kirk was at my cousin's house banging on the door. I felt like I was in a movie. I knew at this point Kirk had no fear and would continue to stalk my family if I didn't talk to him.

Hoping I could get him to back off, I told him I would meet him at the White Hen, a convenience store down the street from my cousin's house. My cousin and uncle begged me not to go; none of us knew Kirk's mental state or whether he might be violent. I had an uneasy feeling about going but also knew I needed to speak to him or he would never stop showing up places or calling people's houses.

At the White Hen, Kirk begged me not to leave him and cried for the entire conversation. (This remorsefulness is a trademark manipulation tactic of abusers.) I had already made my decision to cut things off with him to protect myself and my family, but I knew I couldn't state it that plainly to him or I'd risk one of his explosive episodes. I led him to believe that everything was okay between us. But after that day, I did everything I could to ignore him and avoid him. I went for weeks without answering his calls or responding to his surprise visits.

One day, after so many of his attempts to see me, I gave in and told him I would meet him. Since some time had passed, I began to wonder if maybe I had overreacted. I convinced myself that it was just that one event, that one episode, and maybe he wasn't a bad guy. He was still the guy who had bought me that ring, wasn't he? I did feel that he really loved me, even though hurt people hurt people.

Kirk was both. He was the guy who had bought me the ring. But he was also the guy who made up outrageous stories to convince me to stay and who had raped me. I just couldn't reconcile these versions of him or how to feel about him. It was confusing. Regardless, Kirk was the one person who had an insane hold on me.

I agreed to go with him and a few of his friends to the basketball court where they were going to shoot hoops and play a game of shirts versus skins. It was a hot day, and as the game dragged on, I could tell Kirk was sweating profusely. I couldn't understand why he hadn't taken his shirt off yet, because it was drenched with sweat. The rest of his shirts team had already abandoned their tees to a pile on the side of the court.

Once he was finally too hot to withstand his damp T-shirt, he stripped it off. That's when I saw it.

There on his shoulder was a brand-new tattoo—the name of his ex-girlfriend. The sting of jealousy erupted inside me; I didn't know I could get that mad. Every cuss word and bad name came spilling out of me. I could feel my face flushed with fury as I pointed my finger right into his chest and lost it on him in front of his friends. Despite the difference in our size, I even swung at him a few times.

In this fit of rage, trying to rationalize his betrayal, Kirk reminded me this was all *my* fault for ignoring him. I had pushed him in his ex-girlfriend's direction. If only I had taken his calls and paid him attention, he wouldn't have gone back to his ex. He turned the entire situation on me. This time I could see how manipulative he was. I was finally done; I was over him.

CHAPTER SEVEN

We Were All Lost

1994–1995
Orland Park, Illinois

WHEN A NEW school year began, I started hanging out with a new crew. A girl named Nancy became my new best friend. We met through Isabel's ex-boyfriend. She was my age, was quite tall with an average build, and had buck teeth. Like me, she was a rebellious girl who didn't care about anything. In fact, she was completely out of control and did whatever she wanted, especially since her dad provided no supervision. My dad at least cared enough to try to curb my rebellious spirit.

I'll say one thing about Nancy: she certainly knew how to throw a party. Her parents were almost never at home, so she had a party at her house every week. I never missed one.

During this period, I played my parents against each other. I was straddling homes, staying with my mom a lot of the time and my dad's the rest of the time. If one upset me,

I'd go to the other's house. It was harder for either of them to track my whereabouts when I could be at either place.

Then one week, I stayed at Nancy's house without giving either my mother or father any word about my whereabouts. On the seventh day, my mother finally showed up at Nancy's, threatening her parents for harboring a runaway. Nancy's father told me I had to leave immediately and that I was no longer welcome at their house. I reluctantly got into my mother's car and then noticed the back seat was filled with hampers of clothes—*my* clothes.

As she started driving, I noticed that we were not headed toward her house. Instead, my very own mother had ambushed me, driving me straight to the police station. Soon afterward, an ambulance arrived, and I was forcibly strapped down and immediately taken to Hartgrove Hospital for inpatient psychiatric treatment. I didn't see this coming and felt completely panicked, as anyone would be. I had no idea my mother was capable of such a plan.

After my first week of hospitalization, I received a phone call from my dad. I was happy to hear his voice and could tell he was happy to hear mine. Then I heard his sigh of relief, knowing I was safe and sound, which abruptly shifted the happy mood.

It turned out he had absolutely no idea where I had been. My mother had set up my admission into Hartgrove without his knowledge, much less his permission, so he felt totally betrayed. *Join the club*, I remember thinking.

Even with my mother's extreme betrayal, I had decided I would have to make the best of my situation. Instead of screaming and yelling for the duration of my time there— which at that point was still undetermined—I decided to take my punishment in stride. Having already been in lockup here previously, I knew the drill.

The fastest way out was to cooperate. So during this stay I became an advocate of my own well-being, participating in every group I had to. I knew that if I did not actively begin to show signs of some improvement, I might be locked up indefinitely, or at least that's how it felt at the time. This was obviously not what I wanted, so I became the model patient, attempting to show them my better qualities.

I had been there a few weeks and still didn't know how much longer it would be before I was allowed to go home. I participated in everything they recommended, did all my homework assignments, and engaged with swimming, playing sports, and showing up at movie nights. If they named it, I did it.

Eventually, I was allowed to go outside where we could sit. The smell of the air was incredible. I could hear the sounds of the cars bumping, their speakers pounding out music as they drove by the privacy fence. That sound made me so homesick for my everyday life. I could not wait to get out of there.

* * * * *

Each week that passed, I became increasingly more homesick and far less tolerant of being there. Dad had continued to call and check in on me periodically, and each time I begged him to let me come home. I told him that I was now much better and that I wouldn't be any more trouble for him. He fed me the same line every time, saying he would speak to my counselor and see what she thought.

One time I was so desperate to go home that hearing this canned response made me desperate. I began to cry uncontrollably. "I just want to go home!"

I knew I needed to try to keep my wailing and begging to a minimum. Any emotional outbursts around there meant I might be restrained. There was a nurse sitting right there in the room, giving me the side-eye as I cried into the receiver. But the more he stalled on giving me the only answer I would tolerate, the more carried away I became, and the more the nurse glared. She started to move to the edge of her seat, ready to pounce.

"They're going to restrain me if you don't come get me. Is that what you want?!" I screamed, trying to appeal to him through dramatic desperation.

The nurse stood and came over to me. I braced myself for some kind of submission maneuver, but instead she took the phone away and ended the conversation with my dad.

Later that night, they had my bed moved into the hallway so that they could observe me. It hadn't been the first time that a staff member observed a desperate teenager explode at a parent for putting them in Hartgrove. Some patients had even taken their own lives because of it. As a result, the nurses and staff wheeled beds out of private rooms and used restraints any time they were particularly worried about a patient's potential for self-harm. I wasn't suicidal in the least, but it was protocol—move the bed out, observe carefully. What do you think this does to a person's dignity? Thankfully, I was not held in restraints.

As I laid there that night, all I could think about was the conversation with my father. I wondered if he believed that I had really changed, if he would come get me, if he really would talk to my counselor.

More time passed.

I continued going to the required sessions and doing my homework, but I had lost motivation to participate in activities, feeling like it wasn't really producing the result I wanted, which was my release. I spent a lot of time laying in my room alone, cut off from both my parents and everyone else.

In the earliest days of being admitted, I had missed my friends terribly and spent a lot of time wondering what they were all up to and whether they were wondering where I had gone. But as time passed, I became so detached that I eventually stopped thinking about them or what a reunion with them would be like. It only depressed me.

I didn't dream much about what freedom would be like either, because I could see no end to what I viewed as my imprisonment. To me, it was horrific. I became hopeless and despondent. Some weeks I had a hard time telling what day it was since every day was the same schedule, the same four walls. It was like time just stopped altogether.

I became zombielike, just going through the motions while following the direction of the staff. I couldn't afford to commit a single infraction; if I stepped out of line, it would only prolong my stay. So I laid low, just trying to make it through another day without doing anything to irritate the nurses.

And then around day forty-five, I was to be set free.

My parents arrived at the hospital to bring me home. They must have gotten reports about how compliant I had become, that I was now recovered enough to return to my regular life. But their having me discharged had nothing to do with my progress.

I was ecstatic about getting my freedom back and escaping that institution once and for all. During those early days after my release, I thought a lot about people who were mentally ill and held in psychiatric facilities for months or even years. My sense of empathy, even as a teenager, was quite strong. I began to wonder how hard it must be for patients to readjust to life after being locked away for so long.

Even for a teenager like me, who had been in the hospital for only about six weeks, it was surreal returning to an environment without lockup wards or watching people being forced to take their medications. The staff at Hartgrove had certainly wanted me on medication, too, but I refused. I told my parents I drew the line there. Still, every day, I'd watch the nurses come around for med check and stand with their little Dixie cups on a tray, pass the cup to the patient, and watch them swallow. Then they'd check under their tongues and inside their cheeks to make sure the pills had actually been ingested.

I could only imagine how difficult it would be for an adult to return to life after being cut off from their friends and family, deemed "crazy" by everyone. One thing was certain, I had come out with a new perspective on life, and I knew that no matter what happened, I did not want to end up back there ever again.

*   *   *   *   *

Despite not wanting to ever give my parents cause to send me back to Hartgrove, it wasn't enough to keep me from trouble. I was reckless and uncaring. I returned to Benjamin Braun. I returned to hanging out with Carol and Nancy, while I also got close with a new kid that went there too. Mark was a Greek kid from the South Side of Chicago who spent a lot of his time in Englewood, one of the roughest neighborhoods in Chicago. So it wasn't a surprise to find out that Mark was a member of a local gang called The Devil's Soldiers. And since I was fearless (on top of being reckless and uncaring), I started hanging out and using drugs with them too.

Mark and I became best friends, and eventually this

blossomed into a relationship. Our relationship was never really set up for success, because his parents hated me. They wanted him to date a Greek girl. I also wasn't wanting a relationship that was too serious and committed.

As summer approached, I planned to go spend it with my mom, who had bounced back to Tennessee to be with her ex-husband. He got upset and told me that he would not be waiting for me when I got back. Then, I didn't end up going. When I told him my plans changed, he said he was heading to Greece for the summer. I told him that I would not be waiting around for him when he got back. That was that. We broke up and went our separate ways. He headed to Greece.

Yet since I stuck around and I already knew Mark's friends, I started hanging out with them instead. He didn't need to be home for me to hang out with the people he already introduced me to. Those friends introduced me to a couple of girls they also hung out with, Shelly and Abby. Abby and I became very close friends. In fact, we are still friends now, albeit living very different lives.

The summer turned into a daze, a complete escape from reality. Every night we'd get messed up, smoking dunked squares until six in the morning. As we cruised around the neighborhoods day after day, I learned how to sell drugs and started selling my own stash. I sold acid mostly and sometimes cocaine and weed. I'd roll back home in my car, and it'd be shot up with bullet holes and stink of booze and drugs.

My dad's new girlfriend, Mary, knew something was horribly wrong and convinced my dad to follow me one day.

He hired a PI, who saw me driving into rough neighborhoods. Dad worked out the rest from there but never really confronted me or intervened. At that point I think he had decided I was a lost cause and there was nothing more he could do. I was just going to have to figure it out or end up dead. I'm still not sure how the latter never happened.

One day we took a ride over to Abby's house to check on her little sister, Lucy. We hung out, and Abby's mom smoked a joint with us, which was fun for a while, laughing at nothing. Abby's mom was deaf, and we were tripping so hard Abby couldn't even understand her mother's signs. At first it was funny, but then her mom went ballistic, for reasons I never understood. She ended up screaming at us and chasing us out of the house.

The next day when I went to pick Abby up from her house, she told me their mom had left for good—she just abandoned Abby and Lucy. Since Abby's mom had left before, they had a plan. Lucy was able to stay with her previous foster mom, Rebecca, and Abby was able to stay with one of our other friends.

Watching Abby execute a ready-made plan for the possibility their mom might abandon them made me realize how messed up other people's lives were. Many of the young people in my life were dealing with difficult family situations further complicated by poverty, substance abuse, alcoholism, domestic violence, or some combination of them all. Life wasn't easy or kind to any of us. We were just kids, and our parents weren't showing up. This left us to our own devices. Looking back, I realize how lost we all were—us kids and our parents. None of us were all right, or all put together, or making the best choices. We were making it up as we went, doing the best we could with whatever we had.

Part Two

CHAPTER EIGHT

Crossroads

1995–1997
Oak Park, Illinois

SOMEHOW, DESPITE MY continued rebellion, I scraped by and made it to high school graduation. My junior and senior years I was mostly left to my own devices. My dad had become very preoccupied with Mary, which meant he paid less attention to my extracurricular activities.

By the time graduation rolled around, I felt Dad and I were coming to a crossroads. I could tell he and Mary were ready to take the next step and move in together, and I wasn't sure about how all that might play out. I just had the feeling she might throw me out.

As I suspected, Dad put his condo up for sale, and they moved in together. The condo sold right away, and the next thing I knew I was packing to move to Mary's.

Mary went over her rules with me. One of these was no boyfriends in the room with the door closed. "Will do," I told her. I still wasn't sure that even if I did follow the rules things would go well.

I let Dad know that I was concerned about all of us moving in together. I was convinced Mary and I were one argument away from her throwing me and my brother out. Mary's daughter would only add to the impending dumpster fire. He brushed me off, saying everything would be fine.

With nowhere else to go, I moved my stuff in; I was still his daughter, and I didn't have a plan yet for what life looked like after graduation. It was amazing I even graduated at all, and somewhere deep inside me I had hoped that would make him proud. Maybe it would help him see I was capable when I applied myself.

The day I moved in, I got into an argument with Mark, who was helping me move my stuff in. We were an on-and-off-again kind of couple. That day he was upset that I was leaving for the weekend to party with Abby. We were going to throw a party at the home of her foster mom while she was gone. He didn't want me to go. We kept our voices low so no one knew what I was getting up to.

We wanted to finish our conversation where no one could hear us, so we stepped into the doorjamb of my room, where we could get some privacy while I also tried to respect the rule of having no boys behind closed doors. Mary's thirteen-year-old daughter appeared outside the door and stood there watching us. I shooed her away with my hands.

She wasn't picking up on my social cues. "Can you give

us a second?" I asked her. "I'm trying to talk to my boyfriend."

"No," she replied with her nose turned up, practically stepping into the room with us. "This is my house. I don't have to go anywhere."

"I'm just asking you for a few minutes. Get away from the door, okay?"

"No," she said, glaring at me.

I grabbed her shoulders and forced her to take a step back. She stepped back into the doorway. I picked her up and put her outside the door and then closed it. All I wanted to do was finish my conversation.

Mary came running, of course, screaming at the top of her lungs like I had committed a felony. "I told you, NO boys in rooms with CLOSED doors!"

"Chill out. I was only trying to finish a conversation, and this brat wouldn't give me some space."

Mary made some backhanded comment about the "kinds of things" I might do behind a closed door, implying that I was a slut.

"Fuck you, bitch," I snapped, not thinking twice before the words left my mouth.

My dad was suddenly there between us, completely useless.

"Are you going to let her talk to me like that?" Mary asked him.

"He can't stop me," I said just loud enough for her to hear it.

"Get the fuck out of my house," she seethed.

I turned to my dad, ignoring Mary's death glare. "I told you this was going to happen. I didn't even make it one day."

He sighed, shaking his head from side to side, totally defeated.

Yes, I had graduated, and I should have behaved more maturely. Yet there was some part of me that still felt like that four-year-old who had been abandoned by her parents. I still craved the love of my family.

I missed the family that used to sit together at dinner and went to carnivals to sell balloons—the family with parents working as a team, who invested in their children's education, health, and well-being. I just wanted my parents to care about me and put my needs before their own. I could see that my dad had tried this for years but to no avail; I had been relentless in my pursuit of all the wrong things, no matter what he or my mother did. They couldn't save me.

I stared Mary down, trying to hold my ground. Maybe if I didn't say anything she would calm down and change her mind. But then she held her hand out, palm up. "Give me the house key. You're not welcome here."

I knew I had lost. I knew my dad wasn't going to defend me or beg her to let me stay.

"No problem," I responded sharply, "But I'm keeping the key until I find a place to put all my things."

It was clear in this moment I was on my own and the only person I could truly depend on was myself.

After I got kicked out, I was more or less homeless for

a month, couch-surfing to get by. Mom hadn't returned from Tennessee (though she would), so I obviously couldn't stay with her. So I was at Rebecca's house with Abby and Lucy for a few days, until we *did* throw a party, someone threw up over the balcony, and we got kicked out. Then, I went over to another friend's house, but I needed a more long-term living situation.

Toward the end of the month, my mom came back to the area, but she had moved in with my grandmother. This left no room for me. So I went to my other grandmother's place for a bit, but there wasn't enough space there either. Dad and Mary had gotten into an argument after Mary kicked me out, and he had moved in temporarily with his mother.

I went to live with my maternal grandmother and dad for a few days. But that was also short-lived as I gave my friend a hair scrunchie, and she told the family it was a baggie with a twist tie, which made her think I had drugs in her house. When she shared it with the whole family, I felt that I would rather be homeless than stay there. Interally, my system refused to take the treatment they wanted to give me. It was like I knew better, even though I am now seeing the damage today.

The whole thing felt maddening. The bouncing from place to place wasn't realistic, and not having a space to call my own was disheartening. I didn't feel truly wanted anywhere I went.

Abby and I cooked up a plan to get an apartment together. This was way harder than either of us thought it would be. In hindsight, it's no wonder. We were two messed up teenagers with no plan, no money, no references. Because I didn't have the full amount for a deposit or first month's rent, my dad offered me some money so I could sign the lease.

Abby and I rented a one-bedroom apartment on Madison and Scoville in Oak Park for the two of us plus Abby's sister, Lucy, who was finishing up high school. (Their mom had never returned.) We turned the dining room into another bedroom so they could have one room and I could have the other.

It's hard to imagine how we managed that kind of independence or how we convinced the landlord to allow us to rent from him when none of us had jobs and we were barely eighteen. The universe must've been on our side, because right after we moved in, Abby and I found two jobs we could walk to from the apartment.

Abby started working as a gas station attendant, and I started working as a switchboard operator at a car dealership. The biggest perk was that my employers helped me get a cheap used car by deducting a little bit each month from my paycheck. It wasn't the most glamorous job, but I was bringing in my own money and supporting myself. Plus, I now had a car. I didn't know it then, but this job would be the entry into a business where I would spend several years of my life, one that would have a significant impact on me professionally.

At age eighteen, I was so proud of having a place of my

own and working a stable job. Yet our time at that apartment was short-lived. I hadn't changed much about my social life. I was still using drugs recreationally and partying all the time. The neighbors were complaining about our unruly behavior, and there was no way the management was going to let us stay. Sadly, the constant smell of marijuana coming from our unit and the excessive partying resulted in our eventual eviction. We had been there only about six months. But this was a critical part in my journey, the first big step in my independence. I still had a lot to learn.

Rebecca lived down the street from us, and after she heard what happened, she let me and Lucy stay with her for a bit. Abby, on the other hand, had learned she was pregnant around the time we were evicted, so she moved in with her then boyfriend, Tim.

Yet again, I had to rely on staying in someone else's home. I missed having my own space and was beginning to tire of the feeling that I was always drifting around, trying to find my place. I was grateful to have a roof over my head, but Rebecca didn't really want me there. After all, this woman didn't owe me anything. It wasn't like she was *my* foster mom. I knew I would need to leave eventually, so as soon as I settled in, I began to figure out where my next place would be.

The uncertainty of my living situation made it stressful to hold down my switchboard job at the dealership, so I quit. Lucy and I found a three-bedroom apartment with a huge kitchen and family room. It was only $600 a month in the

Brighton Park neighborhood on Talman. We moved in with a third friend, Patricia.

When we moved into the new apartment, we realized that some members of The Devil's Soldiers were living right next door. I recognized one of them, Pancho. He was a friend of Mark's. I knew Soldiers would come over whenever they wanted and take whatever they wanted, so we wanted to keep a low profile and hide our comings and goings so they wouldn't notice us.

That night after settling in, we heard someone breaking a window in the front of the building. When we looked outside, we realized it was one of the Bouras guys—Rico, a guy I had a personal and romantic history with—and his crew. Before we could stop her, Lucy opened the front door. "Rico?"

We chatted for a few minutes, keeping it cool, and then locked ourselves back inside. We really didn't want the Bouras guys to know where we lived because then they would stop by whenever they wanted a place to chill. And if we had our boyfriends over, they would not care at all and act like they owned the place. I wasn't really that interested in getting messed up with them. At least not intentionally.

The next day, I saw one of Pancho's friends riding a bike in front of our apartment. He was known to the Devil's Soliders as Ace, but his birth name was Connor, and that's what I came to call him. I thought he was kind of cute. He was Latino with a dark complexion, dark hair and eyes, and deep dimples. As I chatted with Pancho outside, Connor showed off on his bike, clearly trying to get my attention. They asked us what we were doing later that night, saying they wanted to come by and drink. We agreed, thinking that sounded fun.

But later that night, just as the Soldiers arrived at our place, the boys we knew from their rival gang, the Bouras guys, pulled up too. My stomach dropped when I saw them.

Somehow, even with eight million people living in Chicago, it still felt like too small a world. There we were, all standing outside of the apartment on the stoop. This was a recipe for disaster.

The Bouras guys wanted to trip on acid with us, and we knew they wouldn't care what we said—they'd do what they wanted. We knew the danger we were putting ourselves in with rival gangs hanging out in our apartment.

So, there we were in our new apartment. The Bouras guys were hanging out in my room. The Soldiers were in the living room. There was not enough room for all of us (literally or figuratively).

Everything started off fine, but things turned quickly.

An argument broke out in the living room over something stupid, and one of the Soldiers threw a bottle from across the room, hitting Lucy in the head, busting the flesh on her scalp wide open. She started bleeding everywhere. Then one of our neighbors, a Soldier, pulled out a gun and held it up to the head of one of the Bouras guys, threatening to pull the trigger.

In my panic, I chose a fight response and immediately sandwiched myself between them. We were standing there like we were trapped in a crowded elevator.

Soldier Pancho's chest moved in and out against mine as he looked over my head to Bouras Nicky's forehead behind me. Nicky's chest was pressed into my back, and I could feel his heart thumping against my shoulder blades. Pancho held the long-barreled .357 revolver up against my left ear. If he shot, I would have become permanently deaf in that ear and Nicky's brains would have exploded all over me.

Again, without thinking, I raised my hand and wrapped my fingers around the gun, as if my holding on to it would somehow prevent the bullet from escaping and lodging itself in Nicky's skull.

"Please don't pull the trigger," I begged.

Behind me, Nicky taunted him, trying to call his bluff. "You better pull the trigger, bitch."

"Please, please, please," I muttered and shut my eyes. My own heart started to pound, and my left hand started to sweat around the gun.

"You better pull the trigger, because I'm gonna kill your ass," Nicky said from behind me.

Pancho pulled the trigger.

We heard it click—a sound I will never forget. To this day, when I think about this moment, the hair rises on the back of my neck.

But nothing happened.

The universe had my back one more time. The gun had been shorted—they had put short bullets in a long barrel, and it jammed.

The craziness didn't stop there, of course. These boys didn't know when to stop; their egos got in the way every time.

Pancho ran from the house. Nicky went and grabbed a butcher knife from our kitchen. We expected him to chase after Pancho. Instead, he picked some poor schmo with no gang affiliation who found his way into this party. He was just a random guy who was in the wrong place at the wrong time.

Nicky dragged this poor, helpless guy into the living room and pushed him up against the doorframe. He held the knife to his throat and began to press the blade into his neck. The start of a deep cut formed, and blood began to drip.

"Come on, Nicky, knock it off. This guy has nothing to do with this. He's not with those guys." I tried to reason with him.

"Please. I'm nothing," he cried, begged, and yelled. "Please . . . please . . ."

Nicky finally dropped him to the ground.

Then, blue and red lights started flashing outside of the window, and everyone started to scatter like cockroaches when the lights come on. We still aren't sure which neighbor called in a noise complaint.

We had just barely made it out of that fight, and Lucy really needed help. Her head was gushing blood; she needed to get to the hospital. Luckily, Lucy only needed stitches, but it could've been so much worse. Nicky could have been killed. I could have been shot. The other random guy could have had his whole throat slit.

Later that same night, my other roommate hooked up with an older Soldier, and the next morning we woke up to a loud boom right outside our windows. Someone had set that Soldier's car on fire on the street. The flames were as big as the building, and the car was torched.

This was our first two weeks in our new apartment. And we knew the conflict wasn't over.

My life had never been perfect before, but this environment was a new kind of instability.

I was still looking for a job right after we moved in. I had no idea how I was going to secure something full-time with all this craziness happening around us every day. Getting a job would have been impossible given the Soldiers living next door and the Bouras guys also knowing where we lived. I didn't trust my roommates to be responsible, and if I left the apartment, I'd probably come home to having my stuff stolen and any cash laying around completely gone. The worst-case scenario would be returning home to find crime scene tape across the door and a body across the kitchen floor. Getting a job just didn't feel like an option with these gangs crawling all over us.

*　　*　　*　　*　　*

Despite how crazy life was and knowing what bad news all these guys were, Connor was still hanging around. From the night I met him, he spent every night in my bed, even if I wasn't there. Since he wouldn't leave me alone, I got to know him. I found out he had a six-month-old baby, Mikey. Connor and I started hanging out and quickly started dating, or "seeing each other" as we called it then. His baby's mom was not happy when she found out Connor and I were together. She and her friends started making empty threats about coming over to beat me up. When I confronted her, she said the problem was between her and Connor and to stay out of it, but I wouldn't back down. I didn't take threats lightly. I couldn't have foreseen then just how many more years this woman would be in my life.

Once again, I had gotten myself into an overnight relationship with someone. The new factor was he had a child. Surprisingly, I found that I didn't mind this. I loved kids, so I had a lot of fun playing with Mikey.

I always knew I wanted kids and had talked about it often with Mark when we were together. I wanted to have my own family, because I had always thought mine had been so lacking. My thought process was that having a child would give me that unconditional belonging and bond I had always wanted. I could build the family I never had.

Even though Connor had a lot of drama with his son's mother, he was nice to be around. We hadn't really even known each other that long when Connor moved his TV in and started paying my rent for me. It was like one day we met and were talking and the next day he moved in. And with Connor paying my bills, it became easier for me to stall on finding a job.

We had been together in the apartment for maybe a week when his ex came by and dropped Mikey off. Connor wasn't even there; he was playing basketball at the park. Mikey was a helpless baby at that point who needed looking after, so I didn't object, but that apartment was no place for a baby. Hell, it was no place for me either. There was way too much impulsive violence and drug use for it to be considered safe.

That same day, this guy who lived on the block called me, telling me "the boyz" were coming to my apartment to fuck up Connor and Pancho. I didn't know what to do. I had Mikey with me, and it was just me and Lucy. We waited outside to try to catch what was happening and maybe prevent the impending altercation.

Sure enough, Nicky came storming up our steps with some other guys, clearly ready for a fight.

"What the hell y'all doing out here?" he asked us.

"One of your guys told us what's going on," I said. "Please don't do this."

"Why do you like them so damn much?" he barked back, lurching forward at us with his face and chest.

Somehow Lucy managed to talk them down and they left.

I had always been rebellious and lived pretty fast, but

over the last few weeks the chaos had reached a whole new level. I was carrying around my new boyfriend's kid while rival gang members ambushed my house, trying to kill his dad. Not only that, but Connor's ex kept calling the apartment at all hours of the night trying to make him jealous, saying she was hooking up with all his boys.

What had I gotten myself into?

The next day, Connor's ex came by claiming she needed him to come to a doctor's appointment. He left with her, and I found out later they hooked up. When he turned back up at my apartment, she was the one who dropped him off. Moments later, she called me to tell me she had slept with him and then immediately hung up. I grabbed his face and pushed him away from me.

"Get out of my house. I don't want to see your face!" I yelled at him. "Oh, and one more thing . . . you know a few days ago, when I said I was going to see my mom?" He looked at me unsure of where I was going with this. "Well, I was actually with *my* ex." I laughed in his face as I shoved him out the door. "You think you're gonna play me, but you played yourself. Now get the fuck out!" I screamed and pushed him again.

He ran out.

"Never come back here! Stay the fuck away from me." I slammed the door.

Later that night, Connor came back and wouldn't stop throwing rocks at my window. He kept saying he was sorry, and eventually Lucy or Norma let him in the apartment.

The past few weeks of my life had been so traumatic and exhausting. I was like a runaway train; there was no slowing down or changing directions. I was beginning not to care about anything in life or whether I lived, but I also wasn't scared enough to make a change or remove myself from anything. It would take something dramatic to motivate me for good.

Not long after, I found it—something that would force me in a new direction.

Motherhood.

I missed my period. On some level I knew I was pregnant, but for the moment I was denying it. Denial was easy because I took some tests that came out negative. Yet something felt off. I felt so sluggish. Then, awful morning sickness started. I was getting more and more anxious about what it all meant.

Connor already had one kid he didn't take care of, and I knew he wasn't going to want to take care of this one, especially given the knowledge I was recently with my ex. The same weekend the baby was conceived, I had sex with both men. Could I be certain that the baby was Connor's?

Yet a small part of me was also excited, even though I knew life was becoming more complicated. In my heart, I thought this might have been what I needed to finally get my life on track, to settle down and have a purpose or some direction—something I had never had before. The way my life and choices were going, I was inevitably going to end up in jail or dead.

I kept getting negative tests, and each brought me a wave of disappointment. Most people in my position would probably be relieved. I had absolutely no business becoming a mother then, but I also knew that little baby would give me a reason to change my life, to reach for something more.

A week later, I still didn't have my period, so I took another test. This time it showed two distinct lines, confirming what I had been feeling. Anxiety, excitement, and something else I couldn't quite name washed over me.

I was pregnant.

CHAPTER NINE

Meeting My Destiny

1997–1999
Brighton Park, Illinois

WHEN I TOLD CONNOR about my pregnancy, I was honest with him and told him I wasn't 100 percent positive the baby was his. Whether the baby was his or not, I told him there was no expectation on my part that he be involved.

The only two things I knew with certainty were that I wanted the baby and I wouldn't be dropping my kid off with random strangers like Mikey's mother had just weeks before. Instead of skipping out on me, Connor said he wanted to try to make it work. I assumed it was lip service and didn't pay him much attention in the beginning. The thing I was focused on was getting my life together.

I thought about starting to look for a job so we would have a decent amount of money saved when the baby came, but the chaos around our apartment made it impossible to think bigger for myself. These guys were about to kill each other.

Every other day we were in the middle of a gang war. They were putting knives to people's throats and trying to blow people's brains out in my living room. Cars were blowing up outside.

One day, Lucy's sister Abby stopped by after we dog sat for her. Connor saw her walking up to the apartment and started to head for the closet to get a gun, clearly upset and preparing to defend himself.

"What the fuck are you so upset about?! It's just Lucy's sister! She's coming to thank us for dog sitting," I screamed. "Do not touch that gun! She's pregnant."

What I hadn't seen at the time, but Connor had, was that Abby was with her baby's daddy, Tim, and two other Bouras guys. They had all been looking for Connor—they were still pissed about the gun being pulled on them and were there hoping to settle the score. Why Abby thought bringing them our way was a good decision, I'll never understand.

Things escalated as soon as they stepped inside our apartment. Tim stood aside with Abby, while one of them started swinging at Connor. I knew how far these guys would go to hurt each other, and I immediately thought of my baby and that Connor might be their dad, and we needed him. Again, I found myself automatically reacting and immediately pulled Connor down to the ground, positioning his head into my lap while I curled myself over him. They couldn't go after his face or chest if I blocked him. Or at least that was my assumption. Thankfully, it proved true.

They kept punching and kicking at his legs, and I could

feel Connor's jaw clench with each impact.

"Don't touch her!" Tim screamed. The other guys were trying to punch me, but he stopped them. Perhaps he had some level of compassion. They weren't really there for me, and he knew I was Abby's friend and also pregnant.

When I wouldn't move to give them a clear shot at his upper body, they gave up and eventually left the house. They weren't going to get anywhere with me there. As soon as they were out the door, I unwrapped myself from Connor.

Before I could get a chance to breathe, Connor jumped up, ran to the closet, and grabbed the gun that was on an inside shelf.

"Don't do it!" I screamed.

He didn't care what I wanted in that moment. Connor ran into the street and shot at their car. He blew out one of the tires. It didn't matter that pregnant Abby was in the car with them or that he could have caused an accident.

*   *   *   *   *   *

With all that had happened, it's no surprise that our landlord noticed the chaos too. After living there for only three months, we were evicted.

It was well-timed with the end of my first trimester. Morning sickness was finally over by then, making moving more manageable, but replacing my persistent nausea was the stress of needing to find new living arrangements. This felt like a new low point. I had been homeless before, wondering where I was going to sleep and where my life was going, but now I was pregnant. Suddenly I had more than just myself to worry about.

Another life was involved, and time was running out for me to get my life together before the baby came. I didn't want to mess my kid up or have them turn out the way I had. I'd do everything in my power to be the best parent I could be.

Connor and I ended up moving into his family's apartment close by. When he brought me by with a few of my things, it was the first time I had ever been there. Immediately I saw why he had been so quick to hang out in our apartment and never leave. His family's place was disgusting.

They had cockroaches in the refrigerator, and I had to blockade our bedroom to keep the mice out. The tiny pitter-patter of their feet and their soft squeaks were audible throughout the night, which raised the hair on the back of my neck. Apart from the pest problem, Connor's mom's boyfriend was an alcoholic who constantly looked me over and made disgusting comments about me in Spanish he thought I couldn't understand. Every day was a struggle to control my temper with him.

"Just don't pay attention to him," Connor's mom would tell me.

I wasn't going to just ignore another man in my life being disgusting and inappropriate, especially when I was trying to get my life together for my baby. I pressured Connor to get us out of there.

After two months of living there, Connor decided to use some money he had won in a settlement to get us an apartment. As a kid, he had cut his arm open on someone's pool, and when he and his family sued the insurance company, they won. The twenty grand he received had been sitting in his bank account and was our saving grace. It enabled us to rent a three-bedroom apartment just down the street from his mom and sister but ten times cleaner. We got it for only $600 a month.

As soon as we moved in, I was more at ease and more comfortable. I was finally able to relax, at least a little bit. Knowing we had that money in Connor's account allowed us to float for a little while without the added pressure of trying to get a job while pregnant.

Early into my second trimester, I started showing, so I finally told my parents. Given my lifestyle choices, they weren't surprised I had gotten pregnant young, but they were more supportive than I assumed they would be.

Toward the end of that trimester my mom threw me a baby shower and so did Norma. Connor had also started seeing his son, Mikey, every other weekend, providing Mikey with more consistency. It was nice seeing Connor respond to my encouragement to step up and be more present with Mikey, especially with another kid on the way. Things were feeling like they might turn out okay. At the very least, we had what we needed for when the baby arrived.

But as my due date crept closer, Connor and I started fighting more. He'd pick arguments with me over the smallest things and then claim it was from the built-up frustration of not truly knowing if the baby was his. I believe it was a convenient thing to say when he didn't feel like being with me. As our fighting became a regular occurrence, Connor grew more distant.

He started leaving me at home all the time and going out with his friends. One night, I was fed up with it and went out with Abby. Connor hated when I spent time with her, because she was affiliated with the Bouras gang. He knew if I was with Abby, I was with the Bouras guys.

Later that night as she drove me home, I saw all these cars outside our place and could see a bunch of people were inside. Connor had thrown a party in my absence. The place reeked of booze. I found Connor sitting on the toilet completely hammered.

"You're not even fucking worth it," I snarled and walked back outside to Abby.

I honestly didn't think he'd care what I had to say or what I thought about him, but he chased after me.

I had already gotten myself into Abby's van when he tried to pull me out by my leg. He got a hold of one of my shoes and threw it down the street. When I got out, I stepped up to him and hit him across the face—and he hit me back.

It wasn't the first time.

Anytime I hit him, he hit me back. And I was always the

aggressor. Every time things got heated between us, I would strike him, and he would return the blow. This time was no exception. The only difference was that I was now pregnant.

There we were: a young pregnant woman and the baby's daddy boxing in the street. That was the nature of our relationship. Immature and violent. Truth is, I was pregnant, and he was out having a good old time. I was jealous that he was free and clear, and angry that he was cheating on me on top of it all.

Eventually his sister intervened and made him stop.

As our tumultuous relationship continued over the weeks, I noticed a pattern. Anytime Connor was being distant or picking fights for no reason, and I called him out and told him I'd leave, he'd threaten to kill himself if I didn't agree to come back. It was manipulative, but it worked. I wanted no one's suicide on my conscience, least of all my child's father. As my due date was quickly approaching, it seemed even more imperative that I try to make things work with Connor.

This time in my life was incredibly confusing. I was so excited and happy and hopeful to be having a baby and starting my own family. But it was devastating to see the shape my life and relationship were in. I grew up in a family with such brokenness, and I didn't want my child to grow up in the same environment. I should have paid more attention to Connor's behaviors. The threat of suicide is a cry for help, and so was his drinking problem.

Even though we kept going through this vicious

cycle—fighting, me threatening to leave, Connor threatening to commit suicide—he continued to go out all the time and stay out all night with his friends. I had to get away from the situation, at least for a little while. I was close to having the baby, and I had to make some changes.

I called my mom to tell her what had been happening and that I needed a safer place to stay. To my mom's credit, she rented a U-Haul and came to get me right away. I took everything except the bed and some dishes.

A few days later, I went back to the apartment to check on him and make sure he hadn't followed through with any suicide attempt. He was fine. He had obviously thrown a party the night before. People were lying all over the place. I left in a huff, irritated that I had been concerned when, clearly, I needn't have been.

For the remainder of my pregnancy, he leaned on the same narrative: he wanted to be back together, but he just wasn't sure the baby was truly his. We stayed in this limbo until delivery day.

I was pregnant and felt so alone. I just wanted him to be with me during that time. My biggest worry was that I'd go into labor and he'd be out somewhere, unreachable. I tried to stay as close to him as possible so I wouldn't have to deliver this baby alone. My mom was already planning to be with me for delivery, but it wasn't the same. I wanted Connor there. In my mind and in my heart, he was the baby's father. I didn't have proof, no paternity test or anything, but I just knew.

(And later it would become clear that I was right.)

*   *   *   *   *

When I passed my due date, the doctor decided I needed to be induced. Since that would be scheduled, Connor had no excuse for missing it.

I arrived at the hospital on August 5, 1998, to begin the process. My baby girl came into this world the next day with both Connor and my mom at my side. We were all happy.

I was hopeful in that moment, right after meeting her for the first time. I immediately loved her so immensely. I named her Destiny—she was my reason to change everything.

Destiny's birth was a major turning point. Before I got pregnant, I knew I was on a self-destructive path heading toward either jail or death. My life required change, and now I had a new motivator. I didn't yet know how hard some of the changes in my life were going to be or how many years they would take. All I knew was having Destiny helped me peek around the corner and see hope for bigger, better, and brighter things. New possibilities. New dreams.

Connor and I hadn't talked about what our lives would be like after the baby came. I was still at my mom's place, and he was still in the apartment. He had let his mom and sister move in. The living arrangements were still a little messy at best.

The first few days after Destiny was born, I decided to go stay with Connor so the three of us could all be together.

A few days turned into a week. Then two.

Into the second week, Connor agreed to stay with Destiny so I could go out with my girlfriends for a few hours. I hadn't seen them in so long. But while I was getting ready, he just left without saying anything. He left me there with his family, who didn't really want me there.

Not wanting to be glared at all night by his family, I took Destiny with me and went over to Lucy's house. This wasn't exactly what I had planned for a girl's night, but I wasn't going to leave Destiny with Connor's mom or sister. With no real place to go with a newborn, Lucy and I decided to drive around, listening to music and talking.

In the early morning hours, as we drove around, I noticed Connor's car parked on Forty-Second and Campbell. I knew he was hanging with his boys, the Soldiers. We pulled the van over and sat for a moment. It was 2:00 a.m.

Maybe it was hormones, but I became enraged. I left Destiny with Lucy, grabbed the baseball bat she had in the trunk, and got out of the car. I busted all the lights and side windows on Connor's car. Afterward, I snapped photos on my phone and sent them to a guy I knew Connor was with. I wanted to see what Connor would do. When he didn't come out immediately, I realized Connor wasn't even there. We left our stakeout position, and I felt a lot of anger release.

In the early morning hours, I headed back to Connor's apartment, where his family was fast asleep. Then, I got up at around six to give Destiny a bottle. I heard a car pull up in front of the house. The music in the car was so loud, I could hear it reverberating outside the apartment windows. When I peered out, I could see that it was Connor and there was a girl in the front seat with him. The rage returned, but this time it turned my blood cold.

The only thing I had in arm's reach was Destiny's glass bottle. Destiny was laying in the middle of the bed waiting for me to feed her. She was far enough away from the edge. I ran outside and chucked the bottle at the windshield. It made a direct impact and busted the glass everywhere. Connor jumped out of the car.

"You piece of shit!" I screamed while grabbing Connor by the neck. I tried to punch him in the face, but Connor's mother came out and started to hold me back.

It wasn't until I heard Destiny crying in the background that I stopped trying to swing at him.

I realized I couldn't worry about Connor's decisions, no matter how much they upset me or frustrated me. Regardless of whether I thought he was making poor choices, I had a little girl expecting me to show up for her now. The only person I could control was myself, and Destiny was counting on me.

I walked away and went back inside. Connor followed, leaving the girl in the car to deal with the shattered windshield. We were quiet. There were countless problems, but we had nothing to discuss. We were living inside a shell of a relationship, and it was cracking quickly.

Only a few hours later Connor's buddy came to the door. I didn't hear what he said, and Connor didn't tell me anything. After coming home drunk at six, Connor simply got redressed and left again at nine without saying a word. I went in the pantry and saw that his underwear and pants he just took off were in there on the floor. I picked up his underwear only to see he had semen all over them. He had definitely hooked up with that girl.

It was one of the loneliest moments of my life. We had this little life to take care of, and he kept choosing everything else. My shoulders started to shake, and I couldn't stop crying. I didn't know why I was there.

A few hours later, I walked to Lucy's with my newborn baby and asked her to take me to look for Connor. I didn't want to be alone. We drove around some more. We didn't know what else to do. Eventually, I spotted him getting drunk in an alley. I jumped out of the car with the baby in my hands when I saw him and punched him right in the face. He immediately hit me back, and I put my face over the baby so she wouldn't get hurt. His friends grabbed him and stopped him. That was it. That was all I could take. I had to get away from him.

Later that week, as the weekend approached, Connor went out of town with Mikey and Mikey's mom. A friend orchestrated a meeting between them, and before Connor knew it, he and Mikey's mom were heading somewhere for an entire weekend. The minute they got back and he dropped off Mikey's mom, he kept calling and texting me, trying to explain. But I didn't want to hear it. I packed my things and Destiny's and returned to my mom's.

While I was staying with her, I begged my dad to help me get my own apartment. I had hope that getting out of the neighborhood would give our relationship and our family a chance to survive. Connor had been begging for another chance since he had returned from his weekend away and discovered we had left in his absence. I decided to forgive him and try again, and my dad agreed to help us get an apartment.

We found one in Worth, just off Southwest Highway. Connor got wise to what needed to happen for our relationship to work and to be able to pay our bills. He got a job working the night shift at Taco Bell, and I got a job working the day shift. Neither of us had a car, so we had to walk to work. I left Taco Bell after about a month and went to work at a gas station. Then, I waitressed. I found jobs I could walk to from the apartment.

After we moved, Connor took a break from seeing Mikey. It was too hard for me to see his mom come around, knowing she and Connor had an affair so recently. I was really trying to work on our relationship for Destiny's sake, and I didn't feel like I had the emotional capacity to deal with the drama that came with seeing Connor's ex. Unfortunately, that meant seeing Mikey less often.

Then, when Destiny was about two months old, I found out I was pregnant a second time. So many thoughts raced through my mind. I loved my daughter immensely, but I was so overwhelmed with life in that moment. I couldn't have another baby and raise two kids alone without the support of a father. Connor wasn't even taking care of Mikey; how could I add another kid to the mix?

I made an appointment at the Cook County Health Department to terminate the pregnancy. It was one of the hardest decisions I've ever made. I was completely depressed by the choice I was making, even though I believed it was the right one. While I was having the procedure, they told me I had also contracted an STD, undoubtedly given to me by Connor after he had cheated on me. I just sat there staring at them as they told me, putting together the pieces in my mind. I wondered why I was always being treated as less than by those I loved, and it reminded me of never being good enough for my dad. I instantly started crying.

My life was still such a mess. What I didn't realize at this time is that everything in our lives is a message to help us heal our past traumas. Our relationships are mirrors; they help us see what we need to heal within ourselves.

My thoughts drifted back to the kids. I thought about Destiny, about how she deserved to have the best life. I also thought about Mikey. He was the sweetest boy, and he didn't ask to be put in the middle of all this drama with the three of us. He deserved the best too.

In that moment, I decided I couldn't continue to expect Connor to show up as a father for Destiny while leaving

Mikey behind. I set my pride aside and spoke with Connor about how we could make it work. I put limits on his relationship with Mikey's mom. He wasn't allowed to speak to her, and she would speak only to me about pickup and drop-off. This arrangement seemed to work well for our relationship for a little while.

Another improvement was that Connor didn't go out anymore. In the evenings we spent time together or with the kids, which helped us work on our relationship. Things weren't perfect, but I was hopeful that we were moving in the right direction.

Then, when Destiny was four months old, I got a call from Abby. She sounded frantic. Tim had gone out on a drug deal a few days prior, and he hadn't come back. A few days after she called, they found Tim's body. He was dead, sitting in some abandoned van covered in blood. There was money scattered everywhere. It was clearly a drug deal gone bad. Abby told me that this drug deal was supposed to be the last one. It was going to give them the money they needed to move out of his house.

Abby was devastated, and I was devasted for her. Her daughter was about to turn one. Now she was on her own to raise their little girl.

I couldn't imagine being in her position and having Connor killed, leaving me a single parent with a modest income. What I could see was how close we were to that reality if we didn't keep making the right choices. This gave me even more motivation to fight for my family.

For the first time in my life, I started to dream—but not just dream aimlessly. I could *see* what I wanted for myself. More importantly, I deeply believed I could achieve these dreams.

I dreamed of a half-million-dollar home with an in-ground pool. I wanted a summer home. I wanted to go on amazing vacations with the kids. But I didn't want these things for myself; what I really wanted was to share and enjoy these things with my beautiful, healthy family.

Perhaps what I wanted the most (but was least spoken aloud) was a partner who would dream and work with me to make it all happen. The reality was this didn't seem to be Connor. I tried to talk about these goals with him, and he just didn't seem to care. He was content living in our meager apartment for the rest of his life and not moving toward anything better for ourselves—independently or together.

I wanted so much more than he seemed to. Yet I couldn't see a future where we existed apart any more than I could see one where we existed together. I knew exactly what I wanted for the future but had a hard time reasoning where I was in the present. What did it all mean? What was I doing? What were we doing? Were we even right for each other? How did I begin to move toward all the things I wanted in life?

*   *   *   *   *

A year or so after my dad helped us get the apartment in

Worth, we found a bigger place so Mikey and Destiny could each have their own rooms. We found a bit of a rhythm as a family. We started taking Mikey every other weekend, and he and Destiny grew extremely close. I bought them matching twin-sized beds and dressers—Mikey had blue, Destiny had white. Their rooms were filled with toys. Watching them play and spend time together made me think about the happier days with my brother, going to the carnivals and selling balloons and the family laughter and warmth we experienced before separation, divorce, and the horrible new boyfriends who came and went.

Mikey was really happy with us. I started to notice that he'd throw tantrums when his mom would come pick him up from our house. Then one day, he started to hit her and say he didn't want to leave. Although I didn't really like her, I could see balancing everything was getting hard on her too. So I mentioned that we were open to Mikey to staying with us permanently. She nodded and shrugged, mulling it over in her mind. At the time, she was pregnant again, living in her mother's basement with her new boyfriend. Mikey's grandparents were the ones who took care of Mikey the most. They were wonderful grandparents, but Connor was Mikey's father, and it was his responsibility to take care of him.

"We are going to see you again really soon," I said to Mikey as I gave him a squeeze.

Mikey gave up his fight and got into the car with his mom.

"Just think about it," I said to her and turned to walk

into the building. It was too hard to watch them pull away, knowing how unhappy Mikey was every time he left us.

I remembered how overwhelmingly sad I felt every time I thought my mom was back to stay only to realize she was taking off again and leaving us behind. I remembered how disappointed I was anytime I thought there was a chance my parents would reunite but didn't. While Mikey's circumstances weren't exactly the same as mine, I never wanted him to feel unwanted, sad, or disappointed. It was like splinters to the heart.

Mikey was clearly happy with us. We provided more stability for him even though we were imperfect and still figuring things out. I wanted more for Mikey and to do more for him. But I wasn't his mom—not his real one, not his legal one. Not yet anyway.

CHAPTER TEN

Making a Life

2001–2002
Worth, Illinois

I HAD BEEN at Webb Chevy as a biller going on a year, and Connor had been working steadily at the local furniture store. Our two regular paychecks allowed us to pay our bills consistently, giving me financial stability and allowing me to support the two kids. Yet no matter how committed I was to creating a happy family life, nothing at home felt easy. Connor's drinking and partying had become problematic once more. We had slowly crept backward in time, returning to the days when Connor spent the night out drinking and I wouldn't know where he was.

After work, he would stay out super late and get wasted, not returning until the early morning hours. A lot of the time I didn't know where he was or who he was with. For all I knew he was cheating on me, but I never had proof. On the rare occasion when he would come straight home from work, he would start drinking immediately. And once he got started, he never knew when to quit. I hadn't consciously decided how long I would let it go on, so I didn't really know when enough would be enough. Then Sweetest Day 2001 arrived, and I reached my breaking point.

Sweetest Day is a holiday similar to Valentine's Day celebrated in the Midwest in October. On that day Connor went to work and never came home. I called his cell phone repeatedly, but he never once answered to let me know where he was or what time he'd be back. My natural assumption was he was with another woman, as he clearly wasn't spending the holiday with me.

Instead of sitting around waiting for him, letting my anger climb to a dangerous height, I called up Mark, who was heading to Greektown to go clubbing.

"Wanna pick me up?" I asked him. I never got the chance to go clubbing, but I loved to dance, and I'd never been downtown for that kind of scene. Plus, my go-to response any time I suspected Connor was cheating was to act out, mirroring his own behavior, like going out with an ex-boyfriend.

"Absolutely!" Mark replied.

We arranged the rest of the details. I called my sister to come spend the night with Destiny and Mikey. Once she arrived, Mark swung by, and I headed out for a night on the town.

Mark and I had a lot of fun, and there were plenty of opportunities to cheat on Connor in the process, but every time I looked at Mark (looking at me in that wanting way), I remembered the way Mark's parents never approved of me—the way they told me he wasn't home when I called to talk to him, or the way they constantly reminded him he needed to be with a Greek girl. I would never measure up, and they would always be between us. That wasn't the kind of relationship I wanted. There was no point in messing up one relationship to get into another that was doomed to fail.

I just wanted an active partner. Someone who was going to give our relationship the same effort I was putting in or who at least cared about the relationship's success enough to try. This didn't seem like a lot to ask, yet it must've been a tall order because I never felt as though Connor was trying. I certainly couldn't say I felt any other man in my life ever had.

I recognize now I wasn't looking for the right things from the right people. The things I wanted in my relationships with men—whether my father or boyfriends—weren't things they could give. Not to mention I also had plenty of my own growing left to do. I can see now that, at the time, I was calling into my life the things that I needed to heal.

At 4:00 a.m. we pulled back up to my house after clubbing all night. Surprisingly, Connor was there.

"Can you drive me to my mom's actually?" I asked Mark. I knew nothing good would come from me going inside and Connor seeing that I was in a car with Mark. Instead, Mark could take me to my mom's and my mom could take me back home. I was already planning my confrontation.

Mark turned the car around and drove me to my mom's.

As I turned to say goodbye, he leaned in to kiss me. I pulled back.

"Thanks for taking me out. I had a great time. But I'm too messed up with stuff right now to get into anything with you."

He shrugged and leaned back into the driver's seat.

I stepped out of the car and Mark drove away angry, squealing his tires.

Once I was inside, I woke my mom up, told her what happened, and begged her to take me home. She agreed but said Connor and I should talk about it in the morning. I told her I would just head to bed when I got there.

When we arrived and went inside, she waited to leave until I had set myself up on the floor with a blanket and pillow. She was watching me, ensuring I kept my word. I tried not to wake my sister or the kids, who were all asleep across the living room. But as soon as I was lying down, hearing Connor snore in the distance, I couldn't contain my anger.

I jumped up and hid our car keys, knowing he would eventually try to escape. As I started heading for the bedroom, I could see my mom mouthing for me to stop, still trying to keep the house quiet as everyone slept. I ignored her.

Connor was passed out on the top of the covers, still dressed. He reeked of booze. I grabbed him by the ankles and pulled him off the bed. His whole body hit with a thud.

As he came to, I started to yell. "Get the fuck out of my house!"

He shook off his drunkenness quickly and pushed me into the closet.

My mom gave a hushed yell from the sidelines, begging for us to stop and not wake everyone.

I grabbed his face and pushed him. "We can do this the easy way or the hard way, but you're leaving now."

My sister rose from the couch and my mom told her to bring Destiny to the kids' room. I nodded, signaling to my mom to take him and follow my sister down the hall.

Connor saw my nonverbal cues and walked over to Mikey before my mom got to him. Mikey was stirring from the commotion, trying to figure out what was happening.

"We're leaving," Connor barked at Mikey.

There was no way I was going to let Mikey get into a car with Connor as drunk as he was. "Get a ride. Or walk. You're not driving anywhere."

Connor started to look for his car keys. He was so predictable when he was this drunk. I made sure not to look in the direction of where I had hidden the keys.

"I already told you. You're not driving."

While he proceeded to turn things over, swear under his breath, and look for the keys, I called the cops.

When they arrived, they escorted him out and Mikey went with them.

In that moment, watching Mikey being put in the

cruiser alongside his dad, I realized I couldn't live this way anymore. Not to mention how it pained me to see the look of devastation and confusion on Mikey's sleepy little face. His look mirrored the one I probably had on my face the night Mom called the cops on Justin and had him removed. None of us were put in a cruiser with him, but it was no less scary or confusing. I seemed to be repeating all the things I remembered loathing. Worse, my kids were now witnessing the same terrible things I once had, and they were probably feeling just as torn-up.

I was responsible for what my children saw as normal. Up until that moment, I couldn't deny that their normal was having two parents who resolved their disagreements through physical abuse and verbal attacks. These were not things I ever wanted them to internalize or replicate or consider healthy avenues to resolving interpersonal conflict. There had to be some other way for Connor and me to work out our issues without so much violence and without subjecting Mikey and Destiny to our chaos and dysfunction.

I didn't have the answers that night.

Finally, with the house quiet again, I went to my bedroom and passed out.

*   *   *   *   *

Kicking Connor out meant the day-to-day life as a single mom was harder. He had been the one responsible for taking

Destiny to day care each morning since it was on his way to work. If I took her, I would have to go an hour out of my way before even getting to my own job. But I was adamant about finding a way to do this all on my own.

For the first few days immediately after, I rejected all of Connor's attempts to pick Destiny up. I just didn't want to see him. So, I went out of my way to bring her to day care and then turned around and made the haul to work. Even I had to admit that this didn't make logistical sense, so I agreed after day three that he could resume the morning drop-off.

Every morning he showed up to get her, he begged for me to take him back and let him try again. For two weeks he had lived at his sister's and for two weeks he had been hounding me to come home.

On the fourteenth day, I let him beg once more. "Just one more chance, Jen," he pleaded. "Please."

I stayed silent for a while and so did he, waiting for my answer. He knew the life I wanted to create and the kind of family I wanted to build. I just wasn't sure he and I were meant to be.

"Look, I know how much family means to you. I promise I'm going to do better."

I wasn't one for promises, having seen too many broken ones over the years, but I also didn't think one more try could really hurt us. We were like an old car, dented and duct-taped but still drivable. How many more miles we had left before we might totally collapse was unknown.

"Fine. We'll try one more time. But Connor, it *will not* be the same this time. Do you hear me?"

"Yeah."

"I'm being serious. We cannot keep hurting each other and being violent in front of the kids. And I don't want to be treated the way you've been treating me. Understand?"

"Jen, I'm sorry. I'm going to do better. For all of you."

The truth is, all I ever wanted was a family. I had experienced horrible stepparents, and I was terrified for a long time that this would be the case for my own kids as well.

When he moved back in, there was a feeling like something had shifted. He wasn't going out anymore unless we were going out together. We were both working and focused on those steady paychecks and getting our relationship on track. For a while everything seemed almost normal. I still didn't feel we wanted the same things, but I also didn't want to rock the boat.

*　　　*　　　*　　　*　　　*

Later that fall, Mikey's mom agreed that she needed help with him and signed a paper for the local school stating Mikey was living with us. We enrolled him in the school system, signed him up for fall T-ball, and watched him thrive inside the stability we were now giving him. We were all finding our stride.

It didn't last long.

Mikey's mom subpoenaed Connor for child support, which set off a domino effect of custody issues and drama. There were weekends she refused to bring him home, days I was paying for day care when she wasn't sending him, heated conversations where she would hang up and refuse to speak to me. We never knew when we might have him, because she was operating all over the map, using Mikey as a bargaining chip for whatever she needed. There was no choice but for Connor to file for emergency temporary custody since there was no way of knowing how stable Mikey was in his mom's care.

One time Mikey ended up with a broken leg at four years old because he had been left alone and fell out of a tree. How long he had been on the ground with a broken bone before someone found him was anyone's guess. Mikey's mom now had two more children (since the time we originally offered to take sole custody), and Mikey was two years older. He was way more aware of what was happening around him and able to tell us when things weren't right at his mom's place. Given how erratic Mikey's mom was behaving, Connor and I weren't going to allow time for more horrible things to happen before doing something about it.

With proof that Mikey lived with us, that we paid his insurance and day care, and that we had him enrolled in school, we were awarded temporary sole custody. That was only the beginning. We knew we hadn't won the war, so we hired an attorney to help us fight for sole custody. We were never going to be okay with joint custody; his mom did only what was best for her. That sent Mikey's mom over the edge.

One day Connor was called into his boss's office. Mikey's mom (or so we had assumed) had called and told Connor's employers that he had stolen furniture from the company. Luckily, they were understanding. They recognized this was a mother's desperate attempt to ruin any chance Connor had of winning custody. They changed his position to be on the safe side, but he kept his job.

We fought for custody of Mikey for the next four years until the court finally sided with us. We weren't able to agree to joint custody because Mikey's mom could never do what was right for him. Even going to Disney World required a court order. In mediation, she asked for no child support and to claim him on her taxes every year, which we did not agree to. She was ordered to give $30 a week in support. All we wanted was for Mikey to have a consistent homelife and whatever he needed to thrive.

*   *   *   *   *

As we went into 2002, life seemed to have stabilized, which was almost a little eerie. It was hard to get too comfortable for fear the other shoe would drop. Yet I was proud of what we were working through together to keep Mikey. I was equally proud of the jobs we had held down and how we continued to make a steady income. More importantly, Connor was returning home each evening without my wondering where he was. It was remarkable to think about how far we'd come since that Sweetest Day that went so wrong. Maybe we were finally becoming a real family.

Valentine's Day was approaching, and my mom agreed to take the kids. Connor said he had something special planned, and little did he know, so did I. I couldn't imagine what he had cooked up, but for my surprise, I had planned a romantic dinner at home, complete with steak and shrimp and a whip cream bikini for dessert.

We enjoyed the evening without the kids, eating our meal slowly and savoring every bite. It wasn't every day we got to feast like royalty. After dinner, we headed for the bedroom, where the whip cream bikini melted away quickly. We got lost inside the covers.

When we were finished, Connor slid off the bed onto the floor next to me, reaching for something beneath the mattress. It was too small to see, perfectly contained inside his closed hand. He shifted onto one knee and presented a ring.

"Will you marry me?" he asked.

Tears filled my eyes. This was the most romantic Connor had ever been. This was what I had always wanted, and the initial fluttering in my stomach was excitement—the feeling that I had finally attained the prize.

But as soon as that feeling came, another entered: fear.

If we did this, I wouldn't be able to just throw him out if things got messy again. Had either of us really changed? Were we really wanting to do this, or did we just feel we had to?

Knowing that family was all I had ever wanted and still believing that family meant parents who were married and under one roof, I was willing to take the risk.

"Yes. I will marry you."

I began planning right away but then stopped completely as the fear bubbled back to the surface. Prolonging our engagement was my new strategy—a way to bide time while I sorted out what I really felt and really wanted. I just couldn't shake the fact that we didn't seem to want the same things.

* * * * *

Since I wasn't ready to keep planning the wedding, I focused on work instead. By then, I had been at Webb Chevy for two years and was still making under $20 an hour. I watched finance managers around me make over $200,000 a year. As I cut a check for day care each week and watched the rest of my pay get swallowed up by other bills, I knew I wanted (and needed) to make more. With two kids to raise, we couldn't make it on our limited incomes.

My uncle Mike had worked for a top warranty company. Naturally, he seemed like a person who might have information on how to climb up the ladder. So I called him. I barely finished saying what I was aiming to do before he cut me off and tore me down.

"You're not going to get there, Jennifer. You have to go to college or be really good at selling cars."

"I'm not going to sell cars, and it's too late for college."

He half sighed and half chuckled. "Well, good luck then." He was adamant that I would never be able to accomplish this.

There had to be another way. I was already packing the deals for the bank, taking care of commission checks, licenses, and titles. That left selling the financing, warranties, and gap insurance. There had to be a way to learn those things too. I'd show him. I'd show everyone who ever thought I wouldn't amount to anything.

I searched for a class that would teach me how to become a finance manager and found one. I paid for it with my latest tax return, knowing it would be worth getting the certificate that would miraculously "prove" what I was capable of. The course met three nights a week after work. Knowing advancing my career meant everything to me at the time, Connor was supportive and watched the kids on those evenings.

After I completed the course, I decided to leave Webb Chevy and go to a nearby dealer. I started in the office and then one day approached the branch manager, Troy, about putting me on the floor as a backup to finance. He agreed but said he wanted me to learn how to sell aftermarket. I took the opportunity.

I did my nine-to-five hours and then from five-to-nine worked for free for a few months to prove myself. I learned the art of selling all the accessories and add-ons like rust-proofing. Part of my on-the-job education was role-playing with Troy and some of the finance managers. It was my least favorite part of training. Talking to them as if they were customers made me all flustered and embarrassed, and it felt harder than blundering my way through an actual sale with a customer in real time. But it paid off.

Eventually I was selling warranties direct to customers. I was bold and not afraid to ask for a higher price. One of the finance managers told me I was charging too much, and they didn't think customers would pay what I was asking. I wasn't dissuaded. My confidence convinced him to approve it, and we discovered I was right. People would pay. Troy watched as the numbers came floating across his desk, knowing they were mine. What I didn't know was that Troy was opening his own dealership and considering bringing me along.

It was continually bothering me that even Connor didn't understand what I wanted to create for our family. It seemed he was comfortable to just loaf or float by. He never had an original idea or motivation to do more or be more or provide more. He'd listen to what I wanted, smile, nod, and just go along with whatever plan I made, assuming I knew what was best. There was no real conversation about anything. He never seemed interested or excited about anything besides drinking, sports, or playing bean bags.

Clearly we were not right for each other, nor were we headed in the same direction, but I didn't think like this about relationships then. I was in my twenties with poor models for healthy relationships and still convinced that the best thing to do for your kids was to stick it out and make it work.

One night as we sat at home, with both kids in bed, I looked at him. "I feel like you would be fine to just stay here in this apartment forever."

He looked back at me but didn't respond.

"Don't you have any dreams of things you want in life?" I spun the engagement ring around on my finger.

He looked down at his hands.

"I know you know what I want. I want a house. I want a pool. I want to go places and take the kids."

Connor remained silent.

"I just feel like we aren't going in the same direction."

I pushed off the couch with my hands and went into the kitchen. The dinner dishes were now dry, so I began to put them away as I worked things out in my mind.

I'd just make things happen on my own. If he didn't care what we did or where we went, then I would just choose the direction and go. If he didn't like it, he couldn't stop me. No one could.

The next day, without Connor knowing, I used our financial information and applied for a mortgage. I was stunned and excited when it went through. I had taken a chance that my salary and Connor's would finally be enough now and that our credit had improved over the last couple of years.

There it was in writing. We were approved for a house. This was the first step toward making my vision a reality.

We looked in Midlothian, which was close to my mom, who was the main person who helped with the kids in the evenings when we wanted to go out. We found a cute place on 144th and Kolmar. It was a white-framed cape with three bedrooms and a huge backyard and swing set. I was thrilled the kids wouldn't have to play in a parking lot anymore. We even had a huge driveway and a garage. Plus, it was perfectly located—only seven minutes from my mom's house and only one minute from the dealership. I felt such pride in owning my own home and providing one for my family. Perhaps this would be just what I needed to make all my other dreams come true.

When Troy finally made the announcement that he was leaving, he asked me to join him as an aftermarket manager and a backup to the finance managers. To sweeten the deal, he said he was tossing in a demo. As a manager, I was given a brand-new Trailblazer. This was my first new car.

Shortly after starting my role as the aftermarket manager, I was making enough to buy a new Impala and on track to earn over $60,000 that year. The new cars and higher salary were proof that I could make something of myself. A year prior, I never would have imagined owning two new cars or making a solid five figures.

The financial stability I was creating for my family was a dream come true, but it required most of my time. I was working over sixty hours a week and couldn't manage both work and home. Connor's mom came to live with us and help with the kids for a couple of months. Her help eased some of my guilt about working long hours, knowing the kids were taken care of. I tried not to be too hard on myself because at least I was being financially responsible for my family and putting their needs first.

My current success at work didn't just shift my own homelife but also seemed to shift my relationship with my stepmother, Mary. She started to treat me like an equal. Now that I had proven what I was capable of, she was more open to having me and my family around. So when she called me to invite us to Easter dinner that weekend, I accepted. I was even a little excited by the idea of us all being together in the way that big, close families seemed to be on holidays.

Having a closer relationship with her wasn't something I needed, but I thought by getting along with her it would help me to have a better relationship with my dad. Something about becoming a parent had allowed me to see how hard he had tried in his own way. He had always been there for me, even when he made decisions that I was upset about at the time; they always came from a place of trying to protect me. Maybe now he and I could finally have a healthier adult relationship.

When we arrived that Easter Sunday, Connor immediately headed downstairs to play pool. It wasn't unusual for him to disappear and be somewhat antisocial, so I didn't think anything of it. He could do his thing, and I could do mine.

I remained in the kitchen, helping Mary. She chatted

with me the whole time, which was surprisingly pleasant. Dad had bought her a ring but hadn't proposed yet.

"I don't know what the hell he's waiting for," she said with a chuckle and a wave of her hand. There was a naturalness to our conversation, as though we'd been close for years. I began thinking it might be time to finally let go of that grudge for kicking me out. Perhaps she was finally seeing me as worthy and recognizing I was her future daughter-in-law and treating me accordingly.

We had a lovely day, and it is one of the best memories I have of my family together around a holiday. It would have been perfect if Connor hadn't spent the entire day isolating himself in the basement. When we piled into the car to head home, I asked him why he hadn't joined us upstairs for any length of time.

His answer destroyed my vision of a perfect family holiday.

"While we were downstairs shooting pool, Mary's sister's boyfriend told me that Mary was the one who tried to get me fired from the furniture store," he said.

I saw red.

I did a U-turn to head back and confront her, but Connor talked me out of it, knowing it wouldn't end well. When we got home, I called my dad. He refused to believe it or give any credit to the boyfriend as a reliable source.

Over the next few days, there was a back-and-forth of calls, texts, and in-person meetings. Mary never admitted it, and I was convinced it was true and wouldn't accept anything other than an apology, which I would never receive. I couldn't understand how my dad could be with someone who wanted to hurt his kids. Since Connor supported us, hurting him was hurting us. It didn't make sense to me.

As I saw it, my only choice was to remain distant from both my dad and Mary. I didn't need them in my life. Things were finally heading the direction I wanted them to go; I had no time or energy for people who didn't respect me and what I was trying to create for myself and my family.

CHAPTER ELEVEN

Wedding Bells

2003–2005
Midlothian, Illinois

FEELING LIKE I HAD stalled long enough, I decided I should probably start planning the wedding. It had been a year since Connor proposed, and he had been patient, not pushing me to set a date. As soon as I committed to planning, that same nagging, internal voice riled inside me. Instead of exploring what that voice might be saying and what to do about it, I fell into old habits of self-sabotage. I purposely tried to grab the attention of men at work or old flames, thinking that an affair might be the way out without me having to say, "I don't want this." Then, instead of pursuing anything with coworkers, I reached out to Mark.

Connor could sense something was off. He began leaving roses on my car and love letters inside. I'd like to say this dissuaded me from trying to sabotage our relationship, but it didn't.

With two failed attempts to step into the arms of past lovers and Connor's desperate attempts to draw me back to him, I decided I just needed to go ahead with the wedding. The ultimate deciding factor was that I didn't want my children to have a broken home like I had. I would move forward with the wedding in hopes it was the right decision for my kids, and I wanted my dad to walk me down the aisle.

*   *   *   *   *

As the months crept toward the wedding, I started to fixate on things that I *could* control. This created a distraction from any thoughts about not going through with it or how I could call it off.

While looking at the guest list one afternoon, it occurred to me Connor might be interested in inviting his father. He hadn't seen him since he was four years old, but that didn't mean he wasn't alive somewhere or that he was uninterested in the possibility of reconnecting with his son.

"Did you want me to try to locate your father so we could invite him to the wedding?" I asked.

Connor shrugged and took another sip of his beer.

"Seriously. I bet I could find him."

He raised his eyebrows and glanced up at me, gauging my sincerity.

"It can't be that hard," I said.

Connor picked at the corner of the beer label.

"Yeah. Let's try to find him," he agreed.

I clapped my hands together, ready to dig in to the project. "Okay, what's his name? Where do you last remember he lived? How old do you think he would be?"

I was relentless in my pursuit. I asked Connor's mom, and she remembered he had a place in San Antonio.

Over several days, I looked up phone numbers and made inquiries. Eventually we found a rental home his dad owned, and Connor's mom recognized it. We called the number and left a message. A couple of days later Connor's dad called back. Before we knew it, he was heading our way.

His dad flew to Chicago, and we gathered at Connor's sister's house for a big family reunion before the wedding. It was awkward watching everyone trying to fill in the large gaps in time and relate to a man they knew to be their father but who had never been around. At the same time, it was rewarding to see Connor meet his dad and have the chance at a relationship with him. In some ways, I thought Connor could have with his dad what I always wished I could have with my own—a close relationship. I was glad to see them reunited and happy to have his dad accept the invitation to our wedding.

*　　*　　*　　*　　*

On our wedding day, we had an entourage of bridesmaids and groomsmen standing with us. Our bridal party consisted of family. The chairs were filled with people from throughout our lives—past and present.

My dad agreed to walk me down the aisle, and thankfully Mary and I managed to keep the peace that day. Connor and I both cried as we exchanged vows, which was touching. The sentiments we shared made me think that we were doing the right thing and we would be okay. The day was beautiful and memorable.

The biggest irony perhaps was the short dialogue between my dad and I as we walked toward the altar. Despite all my reservations, I felt a sense of peace and comfort on that day. Maybe it was just wishful thinking or maybe it was knowing I was doing "the right thing" by my kids, or at least thinking I was. Yet as I remained focused on walking toward Connor, feeling calm, my dad leaned in and subtly looked over his shoulder at the door.

"Sure you don't want me to walk you right outta here?" He laughed, completely kidding. But that joke did make me wonder if he somehow knew what I had been struggling with for months. Did he have some kind of parent sixth-sense that made up for what I hadn't shared with him about my life? I chuckled at his joke and pushed it out of my mind.

Today I would get married. Today we would become a real family. And tomorrow maybe things would be exactly how I had always wanted them to be.

Wouldn't it be great if life worked like that?

CHAPTER TWELVE

Too Good to Be True

2004–2005
Midlothian, Illinois

I WAS WORKING twelve-hour days at the dealership and hardly seeing Destiny. I was still making $60,000 a year, and that no longer felt like enough. It didn't feel worth the hours I was working or the lack of time with my family.

Adding to my frustration was the fact that Troy had been hiring one pompous finance manager after another. They would stroll in like big shots, stay a couple of months, and then leave for greener pastures. In their departure, I was left to clean up their unfinished deals and back up each of their days off, but I wasn't seeing a dime for my effort.

As a twenty-five-year-old woman in the car business who had never sold a car, I didn't feel I had any negotiating power, but I also knew I couldn't keep working six days a week and carrying the responsibilities of two jobs while getting paid for only one. I had taken time and my own money to get the certification to become a finance manager but still hadn't been given the opportunity to prove myself in that role.

I just needed Troy to give me a chance. I could show him I was just as good as these guys he was hiring. But it didn't seem like that would be happening. It was the start of a new year, so I figured there was no better time to consider my options. I decided I needed to interview elsewhere and see if someone else would give me a chance. I went to a nearby dealership for an interview.

The same day as the interview, I returned home just as Destiny was getting ready to take a shower and go through her bedtime routine. She was feeling my absence heavily.

"I need you to sit in the bathroom while I shower," she begged.

"No, honey. I have some other things I need to do right now. Go take your shower. I'll talk to you when you come out." Working so many hours meant I was constantly behind on everything else—dishes, laundry, groceries.

"No, I want you to talk to me while I'm in the shower," she whined.

"Destiny, it's going to get all hot and steamy in there."

She stomped past me with a huff and got into the shower, muttering, "Goddamn you, mother—" and I knew what the second part of that word was as the water burst out of the showerhead, drowning out the sound of the f-word.

A little heated that my five-year-old just swore at me, I followed her into the bathroom and pulled the curtain back.

"What did you just say?"

She looked down at her toes like they were the most fascinating thing she'd ever seen. "Nothing," she mumbled.

"No, no . . . you said something, and I wouldn't say that to me ever again."

I gave her the look, released the curtain, and walked out of the bathroom.

There was no point in disciplining her further. I knew what acting out looked like. I remembered all the things I had done to get my parents' attention. Now, my five-year-old was letting me know she was missing me. She wanted more time with me. I was too absent.

There had to be a different way to succeed in my job and still have a life at home. What was the point in making money if I had no time to enjoy life or the family I created?

The next day I walked into work, and everyone was looking at me like I was a traitor. Apparently, someone at the other dealership had called and told Troy I had been there interviewing the day before. There was no choice but to confront the situation.

I walked into Troy's office and sat down in the chair across from his desk.

"Let's talk about it," I said, knowing he would understand what I meant.

"Are you staying or going?" he asked.

"I'll stay, but I feel like I should be making more." I leaned forward on my knees and looked him right in the eye.

He brought his index fingers up to his lips while he listened.

"You bring in all these big shots and they constantly tell me the financing won't work, but then I get them approved and they get cars. So when are you going to give me my opportunity to prove to you that I can do this?" I leaned back in my chair.

"How about now?" he asked, spreading his arms out with his palms up to the ceiling. He was finally giving me my chance. "You earned it."

I had a new motivation to prove myself and find the work-life balance I was after. For the next six weeks I hustled and sold. I closed the most amount of loans the secondary finance department had ever closed. But as soon as I started gaining traction, it all came to a screeching halt.

One of the people they brought on to work the front desk was gunning for me, and it worked. He had convinced Troy of a program he wanted to build and insisted that hiring his own people would make it more successful. The fact that I wasn't willing to put up with this man's temper and undercutting remarks didn't win me any additional points. Despite all my sales, this guy said all the right things to convince Troy I was more trouble than what I was worth in sales.

Troy let me go in mid-February and refused to pay me. The $12,000 bonus I was supposed to get for all the loans I closed was wiped away by an advertising expense they charged me. In those last six weeks, they had decided to run an infomercial. The expense of that kind of marketing wasn't originally budgeted and was billed to my department. They essentially took my bonus to pay for a portion of that expense. They let me keep my demo for a short period of time but fought me on unemployment, so I took them to court. I cried so hard, not knowing what we were going to do.

While I waited for the court to catch up, we lived off my tax refund. Thankfully it was income tax time. I knew that it wouldn't last us long. I needed to find a job and fast. I wasn't sure going back to a car dealership was the thing to do. Who knew if news had spread that I had been fired and then hauled Troy to court? The chances of another local dealership picking me up right after that gossip made the rounds were slim. I knew how cutthroat the industry was, and there were limited options within our small market area. I began looking in the newspaper for jobs and once again explored my alternatives.

A couple of months later, we were able to resolve the unemployment issue. Troy's decision to let me keep my demo was all the proof the court needed that the dealership had fired me and therefore was legally obligated to pay my unemployment. The timing was actually perfect.

Around the time the unemployment finally kicked in, I had seen a newspaper ad for a mortgage company needing house financing. It was a small broker shop in Mokena. There were only a few people working there at the time, and the owner was an enthusiastic young guy. I went in for an interview and learned that the job was 100 percent commission. They hired me and I started immediately. I knew it might take me several months before receiving any commissions, but the unemployment kept us afloat and paid the mortgage while I learned the ropes.

I was skeptical about how successful I could be, but the owner said he would train me. If nothing else, I figured this would give me a true opportunity to test my ability in sales. If I had learned how to finance cars, I could learn how to finance houses.

The only thing I had to do in the beginning was answer the phone, but the phone rang constantly. We had sent out mailers to the surrounding communities, and people started calling in quickly. From the moment I got on the phone with folks, I felt completely natural speaking with them. Unlike the car industry, this didn't feel like going to a job. A part of me realized I had found something that I felt I was made to do. I felt like I had a purpose.

As someone who had moved from one small apartment to another most of my life and felt such pride when Connor and I had bought our first house in Midlothian, I believed that by helping people finance their homes, I was doing something meaningful with my life. To me, the most intimate experiences were those memories made with your family inside a home you could call your own.

Within eight months of being in the mortgage business, I made $100,000. I could hardly believe it. Because of my success as one of his top producers, my boss told me I could go ahead and hire a team. His faith and trust in me were empowering. It was the first time I felt like someone else believed in me. I brought on a friend and my sister. I was convinced I could train them because if I could learn the car and mortgage industries, then they could too.

That didn't turn out to be entirely true. No matter how much I trained them, they weren't as natural at sales as I was. I began to realize that maybe I did have a little extra something special about myself that would enable me to reach heights even I hadn't envisioned yet. When I had left the dealership, I felt like a complete failure. But in the end, it was the best thing that could've happened. It led me to this new part of my life, this new career.

It's the things in life that hit us the hardest and hurt us the most that end up leading us to our greatest opportunities and closer to where we are supposed to be. When we remember that hard things don't happen *to* us, they happen *for* us—they become opportunities for us to create change.

*   *   *   *   *

The same year I began in the mortgage business, Connor's dad paid for us all to fly to Cabo and vacation at his time-share. It felt like a dream come true to be on such a luxurious family vacation.

Once we arrived, we headed for the beach. Various

vendors were lined up inside their huts, handing things to tourists. One of them pressed boogie boards into our hands, saying nothing of the black flags raised on the beach. We assumed it must be safe, otherwise they wouldn't have given us the boards. A group of surfers straddled their boards in the water, looking chill about everything. Maybe the flags were from the day before and they were never taken down.

To be on the safe side, I told the kids to wait on the beach while I tested the water. I stuck the boogie board under my arm and rushed to the ocean. I dove in without a second thought and immediately regretted my decision.

The water was rough, nearly swiping my boogie board from under me and taking me down below the surface. I fought to stay afloat and motioned to Mikey and Destiny to stay on the beach. There was no way either of them was strong enough to swim in this kind of water.

Connor figured that it was too rough for the kids but nothing he couldn't handle. He dove into the water to join me. Within moments his boogie board was lost, and the waves started to come in faster and harder than they had seconds before.

One rolled Connor under and sucked him farther out to sea. There were a few seconds when we couldn't see him. He was completely immersed in the dark water.

Finally, his head emerged. We saw his mouth first, agape and sucking in air. But another wave sent him barreling back under. I got myself back to the beach and stood with my arms around the kids as we all stared at the ocean, looking for Connor's head to reemerge. My heart started to skip inside my chest. *What if he dies out there?*

I began to panic, and the kids began to whimper.

We saw him briefly, arms flailing above the surface. Then he was sucked under again. I was screaming for help, which caught the attention of a group of surfers. They saw us standing on the beach helplessly staring out to sea, then they saw Connor pop above the water briefly and realized what was happening. They began to paddle toward him, but each wave only tossed them and their boards aside.

Connor would drown if someone didn't get to him soon.

Suddenly, two guys on WaveRunners burst onto the scene and went after him. We saw them get knocked off once. When they climbed back on, they sat still, letting the WaveRunners float with the tide as they watched for Connor's position.

When Connor's head popped back up, they floored it in his direction, managing to reach him before he was pulled under again. They each grabbed one of Connor's arms and began to pull him back in. Miraculously, he was conscious.

I ran to him, letting him lean against my legs as I kneeled in the sand. He started to gag, and then vomited salt water. His body was completely exhausted and shook. Mikey held Destiny close to him as she cried, watching Connor cough up the sea.

"When I was out there . . ." he whispered to me between

gasps, "the last time I went under, there was a little boy . . ." He paused for a moment. "He reached out his hand to me and said it was my time and to come with him." He continued to cough and shake.

I pressed my cheek to the top of his head and held him.

I couldn't deny that I had my doubts about marrying Connor and about what kind of life we would have together, but I also knew I loved him. The kids loved him. We had made a family together. And I wasn't ready to say goodbye or part ways.

We finished our vacation without any further near-death incidents and returned home, heading back to our normal life. When I missed my next period, we celebrated that our family would be growing. Our twins were conceived in Cabo, and on March 13, 2006, we welcomed Damien and Angelina into our lives.

CHAPTER THIRTEEN

Fallen House of Cards

2008–2010
New Lenox, Illinois

BETWEEN 2005 and 2008, I had made a name for myself in the mortgage business. I had made six figures within my first eight months, and that number continued to rise every year after. Perhaps the most important outcome, however, wasn't the money itself but the additional flexibility I had in my schedule as a result of this financial success.

Finally, I was able to spend the time with my kids I had been looking for all those years working at the dealership. The other notable accomplishment during that time was building my dream home—a beautiful half-million-dollar house complete with an in-ground pool.

That wasn't all. My mortgage career also afforded me the ability to buy my mom a house she could rent from us that wasn't far from where we lived, a vacation home in Wisconsin for us to all escape to, and an investment property that I shared with Connor's sister and her husband. For these three years, life had felt surreal, and I felt I was exactly where I wanted to be in my career. I had achieved the things I had dreamt about back when we lived in that meager apartment in Worth.

I didn't know it wasn't built to last.

Just before the historic market crash of 2008, my boss told me he was thinking of opening another branch.

"I don't know that now is the time to open another branch," I said. He was used to my frankness.

We were already starting to see a shift in the interest rates. One by one, other mortgage companies around us were beginning to close. Account reps were coming into the office every week trying to get us to use them because they had lost so much business.

"Look, it's too late to turn back now. So you either take it or I'm giving it to someone else," he responded.

"I'm the only one here who deserves it."

He nodded and that was our agreement. We went ahead and opened up the branch.

I hadn't anticipated everything that was involved. Being the branch manager meant having to take care of everything, from picking out the furniture and building the desks to hiring people and training the team. I had already learned from trying to train my sister and friend that training people wasn't easy.

Things were difficult. All of these responsibilities took me away from sales, which was where I excelled. Being away from sales meant my own salary started to slide.

Over the next two years interest rates continued to plummet, lending continued to tighten, and the crash was sinking new companies left and right. I took less pay, trying to focus on building up the people I employed, convinced they could learn how to do this if I just kept trying. Nothing mattered. Bit by bit, the company was crumbling, and so did the rest of my house of cards.

*   *   *   *   *

While I kept fighting to save the company, I had no fight left back home. When the twins were born, we had decided Connor would take a leave of absence from work and stay home with them. We couldn't afford the monthly day care payment of $2,500, and my job paid better.

The original plan for him to take a year off with the twins had turned into nearly two years. And during that time as a stay-at-home dad, he became depressed, and his drinking increased. I had always thought he was an alcoholic, so I had forbidden his drinking during the week while he watched the twins.

I thought that once he returned to work he'd shake whatever was bothering him, but he didn't. He would go to work, come home, and start drinking; he had no interest in doing stuff as a family. During the weekends, all he could focus on was drinking and sitting in front of the TV to watch sports. I called him the Weekend Warrior because he'd drink every hour of those two days. I felt I had to control him as if he were another child.

If we had something else to do as a family or if I wanted to take the kids on a family outing, he would give me such an attitude about going that eventually I told him to just stay at home. I didn't need his bad energy and whining with us at the pumpkin patch or out apple picking or at the Sunday matinee. We had started doing a lot of things separately on the weekends. He'd stay home and I'd take the kids. Our family life was splintering right in front of my eyes.

The frequency of our arguments had increased drastically, and every now and then as our tempers flared, I saw the shadows of our younger selves flickering. How many more of these fights might we have before one of us raised a hand the way we used to? Had we really changed at all, or had we just been so deep into playing house that we suppressed everything else?

The only thing I knew to be true was that the worse things went with the company, the worse things felt at home. And the worse things got at home, the more I heard that voice inside my head, telling me I never should have married Connor. I had always known it, but now it seemed I couldn't ignore it. It had felt easier with two kids, but with four, it was more challenging. I simply could not have a fifth child (my husband) to take care of. I needed a man. I felt emotionally lost, the way I did as a child. I began to verbally abuse him the way I was abused. Of course, I didn't understand this at the time. I didn't realize that I was repeating my own childhood trauma and taking it out on Connor.

For years I had told him not to wait for me to sleep with someone else to finally recognize how unhappy I was. For years I attacked him about being an alcoholic. Now, both of those issues were coming up in our arguments frequently. I knew I was being verbally abusive, but I was so stressed out, so I didn't hold back. When I really wanted to hit him where it hurt, I demeaned him for the kind of man and father he was.

"You're like my fifth child. You're not a man. You don't go to work. You don't do what you need to do for this family. We're supposed to be a team." From what I observed, Connor's idea of what it meant to be a husband and father was going outside on occasion to play catch with his son and go to work. He wasn't seeing that parts of the house needed to be fixed or the milk had run out or the bills were piling up. I needed someone who would notice things and take care of them or at least offer to help in some way. Everything always felt like it was on me to fix or save, and I was exhausted. With every verbal punch, I had hoped he would either call it quits—saying what I didn't have the courage to say—or become motivated to finally step up and become the partner I needed.

Adding to the stress was the fact I could no longer sustain

the cost of the house we built. My income had been obliterated along with the market. With no other options, I filed for bankruptcy. I attempted to keep the house, but it was no use. There was no way to make the mortgage payments. The house—my beautiful dream house and greatest wish come true—was foreclosed on.

The mortgage company officially closed. The only thing we had left was each other, but I wasn't sure Connor and I could be saved. My life was in pieces around my feet.

I just can't . . . I cannot do this anymore, I thought as I began to cry. At age thirty-two, my fears had overwhelmed me. And the only thought that came to my mind was that there must be more to life than this—more than such a profound sense of sadness and defeat, feeling so lost and alone. How could this be?

After all, there I was, sitting in a half-million-dollar house in suburban New Lenox, a beautiful home my husband and I had built five years earlier. In the background, I could hear the laughing voices of my four-year-old twins playing in the other room; meanwhile, my husband was outside with the neighbors, having drinks and playing bean bags as if everything was okay.

But it was not okay at all. Everything felt wrong. The conflicts within were tearing me apart. And it seemed as if nothing was ever going to change. My life was at a standstill.

It felt as if a storm had been brewing inside me for months. And on this day, that storm erupted, with tears pouring from my eyes. I couldn't see straight, and my head was pounding. My sobs were so wrenching that I couldn't catch my breath. I thought, *Is this really how my life is supposed to be? After everything I have overcome, is this the result? Is this really it?*

I picked up a journal and began to write my story.

CHAPTER FOURTEEN

Only One Direction to Go

2011
New Lenox, Illinois

NEEDING A PLACE to go and wanting to keep the kids in the same school, we had only one choice: move in with my mom. We refinanced the house I had bought her, putting it in her name since my credit was now abysmal. We packed up our stuff and crammed into her 1,200-square-foot house.

I never imagined I'd be living with my mom again. I hadn't lived with her full time since I was eleven. Now here we all were—me, Connor, and all four kids—along with my sister, shoved inside a three-bedroom house. Connor and I shared a bedroom and king bed with the twins. Mikey and Destiny squeezed into a room, and my sister and mom bunked up in the third bedroom. These were not ideal living arrangements, but it beat being homeless or having to transition the kids to a different school district. I didn't want them to have to suffer anything more than losing our house.

Looking for distractions from big life decisions that needed to be made, I got lost inside Facebook conversations with Kirk. I knew it was the last thing I should be doing at the time. There was already enough chaos and confusion, but I was looking for anything to make me feel better. Everything I had worked so hard for was gone with a snap of the fingers, or so it seemed.

We were living on top of each other, and yet I felt so alone. Connor hadn't really contributed to putting (or keeping) that roof over our heads, so he didn't seem to feel the loss the same way I did. I also knew that there was no way to explain it to him, and even if I did, he'd likely not have much to say or be able to comfort me. Kirk was at least willing to listen and be sympathetic. Having someone who was willing to listen and support me made me realize just how unhappy and unfulfilled I was in my marriage. What I didn't consider was that Kirk had always been a narcissist, a manipulator, and a liar. He had known me since I was fourteen, so he knew all the things I needed to hear, and I was in a vulnerable position.

There was so much I didn't get from Connor, even on the days he tried. We weren't right for each other. We never had been. Staying together for the kids wasn't healthy for them in the ways I had always thought.

For the first time I could see how my parents came to the decision to split up. It hadn't been a perfect plan, but it had been the one they thought might offer each person a better

chance at happiness. It was unfortunate that it didn't necessarily work out that way, or at least not right away. Staying
with Connor no longer made sense to me. I was done living
the lie and trying to make us something we weren't and never
would be.

After a month of living with my mom, I waited for
Connor to come home from the night shift and told him I
wanted a divorce. I didn't mince my words, as I had always
been the blunt type. He feigned surprise and confusion,
which only irritated me. We had been struggling for years
and he knew it. I had made it clear repeatedly. Perhaps he just
thought no matter how much I grumbled or yelled I would
always stay. Maybe it wasn't that he was surprised about our
challenges but that I had actually asked for a divorce.

We had stopped paying the mortgage on the house long
before we foreclosed, so there was a little money in the bank.
I offered him what I could so that he could get his own place.
Connor moved into his own apartment. The kids were hurt—
devasted, really. I understood their pain and confusion. Yet I
couldn't deny the relief I felt, knowing we would no longer
be pretending. I found myself wondering if this sense of relief
was something my parents had felt when they made their
decision to split up.

The other thing that came bubbling up to the surface was
realizing just how little time or energy I had spent thinking
about what I wanted for myself. Trying to advance my career
and give my kids all the things I never had took up so much

of my time, attention, and energy. We mask our pain with money, but when it's gone we have to deal with whatever we've been covering up. We can no longer run away. We have to look in the mirror and fix the shattered pieces.

Everything I had worked so hard to obtain had always been for my kids. Over the years, I had suppressed so many of my own feelings. I hadn't taken the time to really ask myself whether I was getting what *I* wanted in life, and every time that inner voice tried to get my attention, I had brushed it off. Now there was no ignoring it. It was louder than ever.

Apart from Kirk's friendship, however imperfect the timing was, the only thing keeping me grounded in the midst of all the loss and transition was knowing this was all temporary. Living with my mom, getting a divorce—these were ruts. They were pit stops. I had no intention of staying at this low point. Because I knew what I had achieved before, I knew I could achieve great things again. I had already proven to myself and everyone else what I was capable of. Now it was just a matter of figuring out how to make my way back to the top, starting with defining for myself what that meant and looked like.

I didn't realize it at the time, but this was the beginning of a new era, one where I would pay more attention to who I wanted to become and who I wanted with me on the ride. But there was still some drama yet to unfold before I would be able to focus on either.

* * * * *

After another month living with my mom and being home all the time (because I hadn't yet returned to work or figured out what I wanted to do), I could see she was struggling with how much she was drinking. Seeing it every day was difficult, and I didn't want this being modeled to my children, especially after seeing how much Connor drank on nights and weekends.

I refused to keep us where we were, and with nowhere else to go, I had no choice but to ask Connor if we could move in with him. It was an unpopular decision among those closest to me, but I didn't have a lot of friends or any family to help me through this time. They didn't feel it was healthy for any of us since we were still going through with the divorce. But it was a choice of living with the kids' dad or with the poor influence of their grandmother. Connor was more than happy to have us with him again, and the kids were relieved to be under the same roof once more.

It wasn't an ideal situation, but at the time, given how unsettled everything was, it seemed the best choice. We were used to living together and used to our parenting dynamic. The largest difference was that we could now lead more separate personal lives. We could each have our time to go out and we didn't have to report who we were with or what we were doing. What I didn't recognize was that I had assumed these new rules of privacy and personal separation on my own, without Connor's input. We hadn't really established them together, and I didn't know how detrimental it was to his mental health, but that would be revealed soon enough.

Kirk and I continued to communicate, though it never went beyond emotional support. He had been diagnosed with cancer, which occupied most of his focus. We were good supports for each other during a period of our lives when we were both experiencing a lot of upheaval.

I had begun working a job as a waitress at a breakfast diner on the weekends while I figured out what to do about everything. I was starting to get things in order so I could go back into the mortgage business, but waitressing was easy and I made fast cash in the meantime. Kirk would come in sometimes during my shift to keep me company in between customers. I never really told Connor where I was working or who I was talking to all the time. There was no need. He knew I had moved on, but he still had it in his mind that our marriage was salvageable, even though the paperwork had been filed.

In an attempt to bring us back together, Connor threatened to relocate to California. California had always been a place I wanted to live. Connor thought that by moving there it would entice me to go, too, and drag the kids behind me. The plan backfired, of course.

"Your children live here. If you want to be a part of their lives, you'll have to figure that out." I wasn't in favor of him moving to California, because it only reminded me of my mom taking off and abandoning us. But I couldn't tell him what to do with his life, and I wasn't going to beg him to stay.

He would have to make the choice of whether he would be an active father to his kids.

He did take off to California for a couple of months, thinking it would somehow change my mind to see him go through with it. When I didn't change my position, he realized his dramatic exit wasn't going to work and that we were, in fact, over. Missing the kids and finally resigning himself that our marriage was ending, he moved back.

Staying at his place would only confuse him and hurt him, so I found my own apartment before he came back permanently. It was tight, living on my own with three of the kids. Waitressing was barely taking care of us. I filed for assistance to help with groceries. Every time I slid the food stamps across the counter to a cashier, I wondered how I could have owned a half-million-dollar house only months before. It was maddening how life could turn in a matter of moments.

The other thing that astounded me was how much easier it felt to live in poverty than it had living a middle-class lifestyle. In poverty, there were ways to receive support with kids' clothing or with food assistance. There were programs and funds; you didn't have to do everything on your own.

In our middle-class life we had never received assistance of any kind. It always felt like a rat race or being a hamster on a wheel. The stress I felt to work harder and longer just to make ends meet was real. I had been desperate to get there, thinking I would be more comfortable by making more money. Instead, I was constantly worrying about bringing in more.

I couldn't believe that the system was built to make you think that making more would be the answer. It wasn't. It was hard. It was easier to be broke or entirely above the middle class, where you had money to burn. I knew I wanted to get up and over the middle-class hump, but I also couldn't deny some of the ease I felt living below the poverty line. I felt I had been hustling for years. Now I could breathe. Now I could refocus.

Truthfully, the kids needed most of my attention at the time. They were struggling with so much transition and needed me now more than ever. Fortunately, despite getting a divorce, Connor didn't just skip out. At least not right then.

Since all the kids were "ours," Connor and I continued to pool our financial resources to take care of them. Connor would come by at night with Mikey, and we would all have dinner together. We carried on like this for months. We'd spend our days apart, gather for a modest dinner, and then part again.

*   *   *   *   *

Our divorce was finalized in August, but our financial situation was still bleak. One night after one of our family dinners in my apartment, Connor told me our arrangement didn't make sense. I knew where this was heading and silently counted the number of times we had already waffled between households. First my mom's, then Connor's apartment, then our own apartment. How much could any of us take? This was not the stability I had wanted for my kids.

"We are both paying rent and utilities, separate groceries . . . I mean, this is crazy. We should just move in together so the kids can be together and we aren't paying double for things."

Had the kids not heard him say it, I may have had more strength to respond with a determined "no way," but the kids loved the idea. They didn't want the back-and-forth between households. I couldn't blame them for that.

Looking back, I think this was Connor's way of addressing his own pain. I knew he was struggling with not waking up every day to the kids just down the hall or in the next room. The reality of divorce was, and typically still is, that dads are rarely awarded full- or half-time custody. I couldn't imagine if things were reversed and I were the one waking up each day without my kids. Perhaps this reason alone is why people stay married. This was Connor's play to be with his kids again.

Against my better judgment, we all moved into a house together. The kids were happy. Our finances weren't quite as tight. I started to work at my mortgage business during the week and waitress on the weekends. It felt like it would take eons to catch up on debts and payments. Everything seemed either backed up or late, and it felt impossible to save anything because there was always something that was owed. I was in a continual uphill climb and wasn't sure I would ever reach the top, but I was determined to get there.

*   *   *   *   *

Things were okay for a few months, but by the end of the year, Connor seemed to become detached from the reality of our situation. Though we were divorced, he couldn't accept it. He was suspicious and paranoid about who I might be talking to or spending time with, convinced that someone else was the reason our marriage failed. His relentless pursuit to always know where I was and who I was with became exhausting and frustrating.

My theory was that he had been depressed during his time at home with the twins and had never really dealt with it or determined its source. His lashing out at me or trying to blame the world for the current state of our family was just an extension of his depression and the way his grief was manifesting. The truth, of course, was that no one else had broken our marriage or changed the dynamic of our family. The only people who have the power to end a relationship are the people in it. If the two of us couldn't fix our issues, then we were the ones to blame. We must always be 100 percent responsible for our lives.

Connor and I had started a relationship when we were young and hadn't yet understood who we were individually or what we wanted. We hadn't made sense of the world, our childhood traumas, or our emotional capacity. We were just kids when we met—kids who had kids, basically. We hadn't learned to love ourselves before our children came into the world. We were learning how to love ourselves and them at the same time, except I'm not sure Connor or I had ever figured out how to love ourselves.

What I know now is that if adults don't want their children to suffer the same cycles they did, they must be responsible for breaking them. I had a hard time truly being able to do that with a husband who wasn't invested in his own personal growth or in our relationship's. Connor wanted to operate as he had always operated. I could no longer accept that for him or myself. We weren't growing in the same direction. We never had been. His idea that someone else had come between us was false. Our marriage had died a long time ago, but he couldn't see it or accept it. He was more comfortable in his own anger, resentment, and blame than in acceptance or truth. I wouldn't have anything to do with it; they were his issues, not mine.

So when Kirk invited me to go out with him on New Year's Eve, Connor begged me not to go. Because I couldn't let Connor's jealousy and irrational thinking own my life, I went anyway. I wanted to do something fun for the holiday after the year we just had.

I wasn't out with Kirk long before I got a panicked call from Connor.

"I can't do it anymore," Connor said as soon as I answered.

"Don't do this," I said in an aggravated tone, thinking

he was just calling to whine and corner me into an argument.

He hung up on me.

I put my phone down and rolled my eyes when Kirk asked me who it was. He knew with one facial expression. I didn't even have to say Connor's name.

Moments later, Destiny's name appeared on my phone's home screen. She was at a friend's house for the holiday.

"Mom, Dad just called me. He called me to say goodbye. What should we do? Is he going to hurt himself?" I could hear the panic and concern in her voice.

"It's going to be okay. I'm going to take care of this. He's going to be fine. Did he say where he was?"

"No."

"Okay, sit tight. Stay there. I'll call you as soon as I know he's safe."

I hung up and immediately called the police, who had to track his phone to determine his location. The signal was coming from inside our house.

By the time I arrived home, the police had kicked down the door. Connor had tried to overdose on the pills he could find in the house and then had tried to throw them up. I never believed his attempt was genuine. I realized how much hadn't changed.

In those early years, whenever I said I was done and leaving, he threatened suicide. It had always worked. I never wanted to gamble that he might actually do something to harm himself and then have it on my conscience. But he had never acted on those threats, and I eventually came to see it for what it was—manipulation.

Now it was hard to know what to make of it.

I believed Connor was depressed and unable to cope with the change in our family, but not suicidal. Given that he had tried to throw up what he had ingested, I wasn't sure he really did want to kill himself. He wanted my attention; he wanted me to come back the way I always had. There was no ignoring his attempt, genuine or not, but it would not work to repair our relationship. There was no going back.

As I walked inside to assess the situation, Connor freaked out. He began to scream and throw himself toward me, ranting how he was going to kill that guy (meaning Kirk) and tell the kids it was Kirk's fault we weren't together anymore. Police restrained him as EMTs got him strapped to a stretcher and took him to the ER.

I watched them wheel him away, thinking back on how I had once been the one strapped down against my will. I, too, had been committed somewhere I didn't believe I needed to go. Seeing Connor being lifted into the back of an ambulance and driven away, I considered whether I had needed the help and just didn't know it. My parents had done the best they could to help me when they thought I was heading down a path of no return. Now I had to hope that someone on the other side would help Connor and that he would be open to receiving it.

Later that night, he had a seizure, proving he had almost

succeeded in his attempt. I rang in the new year crying and consoling Mikey and Destiny.

Connor was admitted to a psychiatric facility for two weeks. During that time, I filed for a temporary restraining order. There was no way of knowing what kind of mental state he might be in when he was released or if he might act irrationally toward me or the kids. Beyond that, I had to make the difficult decision to let him know he couldn't come back to the house, even though it was technically his.

After Connor was released, he kept his distance for months, returning to his old life—drinking and hanging out with his friends. It was sad that nothing for him had seemed to really change. Perhaps he had felt shackled to fatherhood, which is why he was never motivated beyond occasionally throwing a ball with one of the kids. Anything beyond that I had pressured him into, trying to mold him into the kind of dad I thought he should be. Now that he was truly on his own and away from us, he was left to his own devices.

Mikey was now solely in my care, and he had a hard time reasoning where his dad was and why he wasn't showing up anymore. Destiny struggled with Connor's absence too.

They had only ever known the Connor I had wanted them to see and know. Now, without me there to oversee Connor's actions or badger him to perform in the role of father, he was absent. He was choosing to be elsewhere, and the kids noticed. The kids could see they weren't a priority for him. It hurt me to see them hurting, but I would no longer be responsible for Connor's decisions.

The two things I needed to do for my family during this difficult time were to provide as much emotional support as I could and to get my mortgage business back up and running. I had four kids to provide for on only my income. There wasn't a clear path forward, but I knew I was capable. The only thing I knew for sure was there was only one direction to go from there: *up*!

CHAPTER FIFTEEN

Becoming Unstoppable

2014–2015
New Lenox, Illinois

THE NEXT COUPLE of years were lonely. I didn't yet see it as a reckoning in my life or as being on the brink of a transformation. It just seemed there was no one there for me who was supportive or healthy. I was up against the world, and the world was winning; the score felt ridiculously unfair.

My mom blamed me for Connor's mental health issues, telling me I should have gone to marital counseling and done whatever it took to keep my marriage and family together. She said my divorce would be the biggest mistake of my life. Had I not been so angry and hurt by her comments, I might have understood them differently. Perhaps she was trying to tell me that she regretted her own decision to leave my dad and break up our family. All I heard was that I had failed. I had failed Connor. I had failed my kids.

My friends were still doing a lot of drugs and constantly

drinking alcohol. Some had no self-worth or motivation to make something of their lives. And none of them could understand the responsibility I had to provide for my four kids as a single mom. Suddenly, I realized how small my world was and how few people in my inner circle actually had my back. My sister was really the only one.

Kirk had stayed in the picture off and on, but I could see how his own battle with cancer impacted his own sense of security, and he, too, likely felt alone. He was probably isolated by his diagnosis, feeling like most people around him couldn't relate to what he was going through. I knew I couldn't. Kirk was a narcissist and extremely toxic. But you see, everyone that comes into our lives are there for us to heal, for us to learn how to love ourselves. And Kirk helped me learn that I had to find positive, inspirational people to be around. I had to reprogram the way I thought, or I would teach my kids to do the same things I did. I finally knew that I deserved more in life.

I focused on my kids. I focused on my business. And I began to ask myself why I had endured everything I had. Why had I been surrounded by so much drama and chaos and toxic people? How much was my responsibility and how much was theirs? Who did I want to become? How did I become that higher version of myself I envisioned? I knew I needed to do stuff differently and surround myself with different people. I just didn't know where to start.

Other people's choices did a lot of the heavy lifting for

me. Their inability to hold healthy boundaries in their own lives, or with me, forced my hand. I started cutting people out. I no longer wanted unhealthy people in my life. Before I knew it, I had cut all of my friends out of my life.

We discovered that my sister had become involved with Norma's husband and had ended up pregnant. Norma's drinking got much worse after all of this happened. She eventually tried to stop drinking, but because she had been drinking so much, when she tried to completely quit drinking, it ended up killing her.

I tried to talk sense into Melissa and help her connect the dots between Norma's death and the drugs, but she wouldn't listen. To make matters worse, our mom came to her defense. There was no reasoning with either of them, and I was exhausted trying to talk sense into people who would rather be naive or were convinced I was somehow the problem.

They were the next to go. I cut my mom and sister out of my life.

Months later, around the Fourth of July, my son, Mikey, and a friend drove six hours to join Dad and Mary at their lake house for the holiday weekend. When they arrived, Mary told them not to bother unpacking because they weren't staying. There was a rule that no grandchildren could bring friends to the cabin. It was the rule for Mary's grandchildren, so it was the same for Dad's.

Mikey said they were going to pitch a tent on the property. They hadn't planned to stay inside, knowing the rule.

Mary said the property was also off-limits. So they ate something and then got in the car and drove to my uncle's lake house where we all celebrated the 4th.

That was the last straw for me. I was done. I cut Mary and my dad out too. I realized that throughout my whole life, I never felt good enough for him. I was completely done being treated less-than in every aspect of my life. This was trauma I needed to heal.

I had waged war on my old life and the people in it. It was time to clean the slate and get clear on who would be a part of my life. The only people left standing were my kids.

*   *   *   *   *

While the kids were busy with schoolwork or sports or spending time with friends, I started listening to self-help books and looking for new opportunities to grow my financial wealth. My mortgage business was doing well, but I still wasn't where I wanted to be financially.

An informal acquaintance I had run into told me about a multilevel marketing company inside the health industry. She had just started her own side hustle with the company and was having a grand opening. She invited me and I decided to check it out. When I was there, I was briefly introduced to Johnna Parr, who was also a part of the company.

Johnna had long, beautiful, thick black hair. She was tall and slender, with this chic look about her. But apart from being gorgeous, she had this energy, this way of commanding attention and standing confidently in who she was. I felt instantly drawn to her and knew this was someone I wanted to know personally.

One of my connections knew Johnna and her husband, Matt, and had an inside track. They set up a meeting between the three of us at a local Starbucks.

As soon as Johnna walked in, I felt the same magnetism that I had felt at the grand opening. I knew I wanted to be like her. She had a glow and energy I had never seen in a professional woman. I wanted to know everything about her. Whatever she was doing, I wanted to do. Whatever she was a part of, I wanted to be a part of.

Once we sat down with our coffee, Johnna began explaining the company. I sat mesmerized by her and was hanging on every word. When she was finished, I told her I felt they should know who I was.

Without hesitation, I launched into my life story—my troubled adolescence, my time at Hartgrove, the drugs and gangs, the bad boyfriends, getting pregnant young and then getting married, making great money and then losing it all. I told these complete strangers *everything*. They listened attentively with interest and curiosity. When I was finished, Johnna looked at Matt, sending him a telepathic message, and then turned to me and patted the table.

"This is amazing. You won't believe it, but our CEO, Ryan Blair, has a story that is very similar to yours, and he's a number-one bestselling author. You should read his book. It's called *Nothing to Lose, Everything to Gain.*" I'd certainly felt as if I had nothing to lose during many moments of my life.

"I'll definitely check that out," I told her. I hadn't read a whole book in my entire life, but I knew I needed to know this man's story. I needed to know what was possible for me.

When I left the meeting, I bought the audiobook.

The more I listened, the more I could see myself inside Ryan's story. The one big difference was that he was currently a multimillionaire living his best life and I was still a financially struggling single mom. But we had similar beginnings, and if he could do it, I could too. I joined the company, and as soon as they had their next conference, I attended.

Connor was well enough to stay with the kids while I took off to Orlando. As soon as I was in the conference room, I felt like I was finally in a place where people cared about success. The fact that none of these people knew me also meant they didn't just look at me and see failure or automatically judge me. They didn't know anything about me. There was liberation in that feeling of anonymity. It was the fresh start I was looking for.

Every person who stepped onto the stage was motivational and inspirational. I took pages of notes and let their words sink in. Speakers talked about how to get out of your own way and take control of your life. I think about these messages now and they don't seem that mind-blowing, but at the time they were brand-new ideas. They were perspectives

no one had ever given me. I knew I wouldn't leave the conference as the same woman I had been when I arrived.

When Ryan took the stage, I perked up in my seat.
After listening to his book and seeing so many similarities
between us, I felt like he was a brother separated from me at
birth. I sat in the back of the room totally in awe, soaking in
every one of his words. At this time, I was living payday loan
to payday loan, and I knew I couldn't continue like this. My
family needed me to grow and learn so that I could change
our lives once and for all. I felt, deep down, that this man
and I were meant to do something together. I could feel it.

*   *   *   *   *

Following the conference, I started following Ryan online
everywhere I could find him. I read everything he wrote,
listened to every interview he gave, and watched every video
he created. He became my informal mentor even though
he had no idea the impact he was having on my life. With
every bit of insight and every new thing I learned, I could feel
myself expanding and my life shifting.

The closer I got to becoming the person I wanted to
be, the more successful my business became. Finally, I had
gotten back on my feet. I was able to ditch the house I was
renting and move myself and the kids into a cute house with
a hot tub and pool. Things were finally lining up, with one
exception: Kirk.

I knew our relationship remained unhealthy, and this was the fresh start I wanted. I needed my own place, which would not include him. It was further complicated when Kirk got a call from his oncologist that his cancer may be back.

We went in to speak with the medical team and have some tests run. They said it was possible all was well, but they wouldn't know with certainty until they got the results back. Kirk told me a few days later that they called to say it was back and that he would need a biopsy to determine the severity.

For months Kirk put it off, saying he was too scared. No matter what I said or did to be supportive or encouraging, he wouldn't do it. And then I found out that he had been lying the entire time. The doctors had called and told him all was well. I was so sickened and hurt by how he had taken advantage of me that I packed his stuff up for him and kicked him out.

I finally recognized that I deserved more.

*   *   *   *   *

With Kirk out of the picture and everything on track, I realized I could think more about my goals and focus more on my own financial situation. It was time to sell the investment property I had bought years ago and co-owned with my brother. It had been paying for itself as a "condotel"; my brother and sister-in-law rented it, took a percent, and paid us the rest. Each year we used the rental as much as we wanted, and the kids thought of it as their summer home. But it was time to sell the property and use the proceeds to try to finally get out of the remaining debt I had.

Each baby step toward the vision I had for myself emboldened me to take another. One day I spoke to a friend about the new leaf I had turned over and the visions of grandeur I had for myself and my family. She introduced me to Ed, a life coach she knew.

I desperately wanted to work with him, but when he told me how much he charged, my jaw dropped. I was just getting back on my feet and clearing up old balances.

"How about we start with a dollar? Agree to pay me a dollar," he said to me.

I agreed. I could afford a dollar to get started.

Ed worked with me on limiting beliefs and negative thoughts, pushing me to envision a higher version of myself. With his guidance, I created a new story, one where I was the person I wanted to be and was making a positive impact on the world. The self-imposed restrictions and narrow beliefs were drifting away. Clarity around what I wanted emerged, as did the confidence to make it happen.

I wanted hundreds of thousands of dollars in the bank. I wanted to own stock and properties again. Most importantly, I envisioned myself creating an alternative living space for kids on the streets. The more I shed old ways of thinking, the more my goals began to manifest.

Then, I started searching for a company that didn't have as many overlays or deceive loan officers to try and get them hired. I had gotten wise to the way the industry worked. I found LoanDepot, and they proved to be who they said they were and operated with integrity. It was a breath of fresh air within the industry.

At LoanDepot there would be more opportunity to attain the financial wealth I desired. This is where I would make a name for myself. And I did just that.

In that first year at LoanDepot, I closed nearly $20 million in sales. But I knew I could do more. I also knew it was time for me and my partner to open our own branch, but there weren't any at the time. So, I quit and looked for somewhere else where I could push myself even further.

I hadn't been gone long when LoanDepot called me, asking how they could convince me to come back. I was honest and told them I wanted my own branch opportunity that they didn't have before. To my surprise, LoanDepot created the first profit and loss branch for me and my partner. So I returned.

This would become the place where I would create the wealth I desired. Finally, it was the right time for me to become exactly who I wanted to be and live the life of my own design. I was unstoppable. Nothing would ever stand in my way again. No one could stop me but me.

Winner Takes All: Ultimate Success

BY THE END of my third year (2018) at LoanDepot, my team and I closed $30 million. By the end of 2021, I closed $65 million and our branch closed over 180 million in production. I'm one of LoanDepot's top loan officers, and I went from making $200,000 a year to over seven figures. I have hundreds of thousands in investments. In 2021, I was number one in Illinois for FHA (Federal Housing Administration) lending, in the top 1 percent of loan officers in the country, and number thirty-four in the country for NAREP (National Association of Real Estate Professionals). Every dream I had when I was working with my life coach, Ed, has come true.

Because I've pushed toward my own self-actualization and growth and come to better understand myself and my trauma, I've been able to reestablish relationships with my parents in healthier ways, including better boundaries. Perhaps most importantly, my children are thriving and healthy. Mikey is now working with me at LoanDepot and is one of my most valuable employees. He has his own house and has done a lot of work to heal some of his own trauma. He's a successful, happy, and healthy young man, which is what I always hoped for him. Destiny is now in her midtwenties and living in Los Angeles as an aspiring actress for TV and film. She was just signed to a top management company, and I couldn't be prouder. The twins are now sixteen, thinking about life after high school, and just earned their driver's licenses. They recently got their first jobs, working at the movie theater.

I'm happy to say Connor accepted my offer to pay to send him to rehab a little over a year ago, and he's been sober since. This is the first time in his life he's been sober, and he has a much stronger relationship with the kids because of the personal work he's done in this last year. Through his own income, he's been able to take two vacations with the twins. And, for the first time in a long time, Connor has been in a healthy enough mental state to give advice to Mikey and Destiny when they've needed it, which means the world to them, knowing their dad is available and present in their lives. Connor's now aspiring to help other people like him who have struggled a long time with alcoholism and depression.

Perhaps one of the most exciting things to happen in these last few years has been getting to meet and work with my mentor, Ryan Blair. I had met Ryan on a few occasions and was always inspired by him. I always had the feeling that he and I were meant to do something together.

When he was through his own healing process and ready

to reemerge and begin again, Ryan started a new company, Alter Call, and began offering mentoring. I immediately requested more information. He recognized my name and told one of his employees to get ahold of me.

I'll never forget the day his team member called.

It was a dream come true, yet I also knew it would happen. I had been waiting years for that moment. This team member began to tell me all about the program. I signed up immediately—no questions asked. Ryan Blair became my official mentor.

In 2020, I signed up for private mentoring.

Over these last few years, I've brought family members and friends to Ryan's seminars and retreats. With his guidance, I've learned how to take the money I make and impact the world with it. I've donated thousands of dollars to nonprofits across the United States. And I became the first investor in Alter Call. Through the company, I have been able to heal childhood trauma I didn't even know I had. In doing so, my kids have felt the freedom to forgive me for the things I've done wrong. We don't always know what we're doing that causes harm, but it's our job to break the cycle so it doesn't continue with our children.

We all deserve healthy people in our lives and healthy homes. We all deserve to have our basic needs met. We all deserve to have access to the resources we need when times get hard. We may not all have the ability to become wealthy, but those who get wealthy have the ability and opportunity to share it and make a difference.

More than anything else, I want everyone to recognize their own power. We have the power to create the lives we dream of. We can climb to heights we once thought were impossible. We just have to believe in ourselves and become resolved not to let anything or anyone dissuade us from reaching our full potential.

Life doesn't happen to us; it happens for us. Are you willing to do your work and heal? To forgive those who wronged you? To walk into your greatness and, most importantly, love yourself the way you want to be loved? You cannot expect someone to love you if you are not willing to love and honor yourself.

Stay strong. Keep going. No one can stop you but you.

Acknowledgments

TO GLENN PLASKIN: I am overjoyed with the way you have brought my book to life. You have also been such a friend and guide to me during this process. I could not have asked for a better person to bring this book that is so near and dear to my heart to the world. Words cannot express my gratitude.

TO RYAN BLAIR: Who knew that reading your book would have such a profound impact on my and my family's lives? You have not only touched and impacted my immediate family but also coworkers, friends, and so many more. I hope that I have been able to impact you in some way as well. I look forward to helping many more families break generational trauma, heal, and reach their full protentional. I can not thank you enough for your guidance through some of my most difficult years. Our friendship truly means the world to me. Thank you for believing in me.

Acknowledgments

TO MY PARENTS: I know that raising a child like me was nearly unbearable. Thank you for never giving up on me and believing that one day everything would be different. It is because of all our imperfections that we are able to bless so many lives with this story, and if anything were different, we would not be able to do so. I love you both with all my heart.

TO MY CHILDREN: I know I have not done everything right, and I know that I was spread thin many times and you all wished I could have had more time with you. I want you all to know that everything I did was to provide a better life for each of you, and I hope that I have shown you all an incredible work ethic. I hope you all know that you are the only ones who can create the life of your dreams. None of this would be possible without each and every one of you. Mikey, Destiny, Damien, and Angelina, you are my shining stars, and I love you more than words could ever express. Thank you for allowing me the blessing of being your mother.

TO ALL MY NIECES AND NEPHEWS, as well as all of you who have believed in me along the way: You have all blessed my life, and I love you all so very much.

TO MY FRIENDS AND LOVED ONES: You have all played a huge role in my journey and my healing. I hope that by reading this, you will know no one can stop you but you.